More Praise for
Bill Byrne and HABITS OF WEALTH...

"What he has to say about how to be a success is based not only on his own considerable achievements and experience but also on sound common sense."
—Sydney Perry, Managing Director,
London Weekend Television

"Bill Byrne is a rare breed ... He's got something worthwhile to say, and *Habits of Wealth* says it."
—Jim Bischoff, President/CEO,
Orange Julius International (1983–1988)

"A very readable book that will benefit both young and old entrepreneurs alike."
—Dick McFarland, Chairman,
Inter-Regional Financial Group

"*Habits of Wealth* is an excellent management textbook. It's full of what Tom Peters calls 'brilliant flashes of the obvious,' and that's quite a compliment."
—John Mulligan, Chairman (ret),
American Western Corporation

"This is a super book. In forty years of business I haven't read one better."
—Al Schock, Chairman (ret),
Nordica International

HABITS OF WEALTH

111 PROVEN STRATEGIES THAT WILL CHANGE THE WAY YOU DO BUSINESS FOREVER

BILL BYRNE

BERKLEY BOOKS, NEW YORK

Although the author and publisher have made every effort to ensure the accuracy and completeness of information contained in this book, we assume no responsibility for errors, inaccuracies, omissions, or any inconsistency herein. Any slights of people, places, or organizations are unintentional.

HABITS OF WEALTH

A Berkley Book / published by arrangement with
the author

PRINTING HISTORY
Performance One Publishing edition published 1992
Berkley trade paperback edition / September 1993

ISBN: 0-425-13819-4

A BERKLEY BOOK ® TM 757,375
Berkley Books are published by The Berkley Publishing Group,
200 Madison Avenue, New York, New York 10016.
The name "BERKLEY" and the "B" logo
are trademarks belonging to Berkley Publishing Corporation.

PRINTED IN THE UNITED STATES OF AMERICA

10 9 8 7 6 5 4 3 2

HABITS OF
WEALTH

111 PROVEN STRATEGIES THAT WILL CHANGE THE WAY YOU DO BUSINESS FOREVER

DEDICATION

FOR LYNNE, JASON AND JENNIFER
May they have blue skies and green lights.

ACKNOWLEDGMENTS

Thanks begin with the person to whom I am most indebted, my son, Jason. He has been at my side during the four marathon bursts during which the bulk of this book was written. His word processing assistance, copy editing skills, thoughtful critique, and companionship were a tremendous contribution. His potential for achievement should make the business school at the University of Colorado proud.

To Gene Walden, author of *The 100 Best Stocks to Own in America*, for his enthusiasm and encouragement for what I was writing. Also of assistance was the thorough and helpful critique offered by friend and leader John Mulligan, whose comments made the book better. Few first-time authors are able to find an agent who believes in him, and I'm indebted to Peter Miller at the Peter Miller Agency for that and for his friendship.

Thanks also to Steve Garry of New York Life for his professionalism and knowledge, both of which enhanced the important planning chapter.

Final thanks to my "manuscript mentors" who took time to read *Habits of Wealth* and offer their encouraging thoughts while it was being written. And to my administrative assistant, Pat Rundell, who assisted in meeting many deadlines and commitments.

FOREWORD

You can be a successful entrepreneur! *Habits of Wealth* shows you how by describing practical techniques that will help you gain or develop habits of entrepreneurial achievement. Bill Byrne does not present panaceas, elaborate or complex programs, or get-rich-quick gimmickry. Instead, he offers basic, common sense approach to achievement.

My own entrepreneurial experience has given me a firm belief in the power of habits—the right habits! Avoiding vague generalities characteristic of other books on achievement and entrepreneurship, *Habits of Wealth* provides precise and penetrating information on 111 specific habits guaranteed to generate wealth.

Bill Byrne's philosophy of business is strikingly similar to my own. Points he so convincingly makes in *Habits of Wealth* are the same ones my own experience and observation validate, including these conclusions I have drawn and recorded in my own writings:

- We first form habits; then habits form us. In the individual drive toward a successful future, if we do not consciously form good habits we will unconsciously form bad ones.

- Habits aren't instincts; they're acquired reactions. They don't "just happen," they are caused. Once you determine the original cause of a habit, it is within your power either to accept or to reject it.

- Every person who is successful has simply formed the habits of doing things that failures dislike doing and will not do.

- It is just as easy to form the habit of succeeding as it is to succumb to the habit of failure.

- The harvest we reap in our lives is measured by the attitudes and habits we cultivate.

To my knowledge no one has handled becoming a successful entrepreneur quite so comprehensively, explicitly and directly as Bill has done in *Habits of Wealth*. His beliefs about habits are tried, tested and time-proven. His clear-cut organization and clever presentation make for easy, interesting reading. Consider this sample of typical inviting topics:

Don't Just Know the Numbers, Know the Right Numbers

A Lesson from the Mafia

The Best Promotional Money You Won't Spend

Quicksand Quotient I

Effectiveness and Efficiency: Cousins, but Not Blood Brothers

If You Have Thoroughbreds In Your Stable Let 'Em Run

Luck Is No Accident

While *Habits of Wealth* is written in a comfortable, conversational style that holds your attention, do not let its ease in reading betray the soundness of its concepts. The message deals in habits essential for personal and organizational success. Bill Byrne's discussion and application of goal setting, for example, is one of the outstanding strengths of this well-founded book. The author not only advocates goal setting and explains its importance, he illustrates how to apply it from examples in his own business success and from the successful experience of others. Sharing success stories—as well as pointing out precarious pit-falls—facilitates application of the wealth of practical information in this book.

Bill Byrne

Another extraordinary feature of *Habits of Wealth* is its emphasis on ethics. Throughout the book he respects and encourages well-defined ethical boundaries. This gives confidence to the reader that other areas of this book are equally sound and provide a solid base for lasting success.

Franchising is a highly misunderstood opportunity in the business world today. The chapter on the entrepreneur and franchising is excellent; it clears up some of the common misconceptions about franchising. Sidestepping the usual hazy statements on the topic, Byrne spells out specific guidelines for evaluating prospective franchises. He then follows it up with other concrete suggestions for selecting financing and managing a franchise successfully.

Business capability is evident throughout *Habits of Wealth*. So is understanding and perception about people. Bill Byrne penetrates layers of self-deception because of his ability to *read* people. His discussion throughout the book on the importance of interacting effectively with people and the entrepreneurial leader's success is particularly insightful and helpful. His alliance of business expertise with people perception is a winning combination. The author's discussion in these following topics are especially astute:

Creating The Delighted Customer

A Company Is Known By The Customers It Keeps

The Art Of Empowerment

Motivation In Perspective

The Hiring Habit, The Firing Fallacy

Habits of Wealth is positive and optimistic; it clearly outlines specific attitudes and actions that lead to entrepreneurial success. But the book offers more. It points out some of the problems and hurdles common to the aspiring entrepreneur. This guide probes these stumbling blocks people encounter on the road to entrepreneurial success—and shows how to overcome them. Bill Byrne's "Top Ten Entrepreneurial Mistakes" is particularly discerning and useful.

A singularly distinctive feature of *Habits of Wealth* is that he speaks from experience, not just theory or simply hearsay. His successful track record as an entrepreneur qualifies him well for writing this book. He has profitably founded organizations in several business arenas. *Inc.* magazine annually recognizes outstanding business people; the competition is keen. In 1989 Byrne was named an Entrepreneur of the Year finalist.

As a veteran of more than 700 television appearances, he has an incredible ability to relate to others through the spoken word. This ability is transmitted skillfully to an ability to communicate clearly in the printed word. In addition, Bill Byrne is a living example of all he writes about. His clarity and sound thinking catapulted him to financial success at a very early age. His continued financial success is testimony to the soundness and application of his ideas.

Turning your entrepreneurial dreams into reality does not require magic; it requires a vast array of successful habits. Bill's approach can help you take the gamble out of entrepreneurial pursuits as you acquire, develop and put into practice his 111 well-documented habits. I congratulate Bill Byrne on providing this important book and I commend you for reading it. All the best wishes for your entrepreneurial success as you put into practice these *Habits of Wealth*.

Paul J. Meyer, Founder
Success Motivation Institute (SMI)
Leadership Management, Inc. (LMI)

CONTENTS

CONTENTS

CONTENTS

CONTENTS

CONTENTS

CONTENTS

CONTENTS

CONTENTS

CONTENTS

CONTENTS

INTRODUCTION

If the 1970s was the decade of technology, and the 1980s the decade of communication, what will we say about this decade when we look back from the new millennium? I believe we'll refer to it as the decade of entrepreneurial achievement. A decade dominated by people who think entrepreneurially and by organizations that behave entrepreneurially.

The primary focus of this book is to offer accessible, practical habits that facilitate the creation of personal and organizational wealth and achievement. It uses forms of the word entrepreneur frequently. However, the concepts are applicable to far more than the self-employed. Entrepreneurship is, to a large extent, a *state of mind*. The late Earl Nightingale expressed it so well when he said, "The biggest mistake you'll ever make in your life is to believe you work for someone else." *Amen.*

In selecting the title I was somewhat turned off by including the word *wealth*. Nonetheless, it is highly descriptive of what this book reaches for, especially since *Habits of Wealth* discusses wealth in terms *far broader than money*.

Whether used within or outside of the monetary context, wealth is one of our basic human desires. We can all be *wealthy* if we participate in an entrepreneurial environment. It's the entrepreneurial opportunities in life that allow us to fulfill the three essential human needs—having someone to believe in, having something to believe in, and having someone to believe in us. The most entrepreneurial seek to provide the type of wealth and improvement offered through these basic human needs.

Throughout this book you'll also find repeated uses of *leader*. The criteria for leadership include:

1. *Leaders are people with followers.* That isn't limited to employees. It refers to anyone having a destination someone else also wants to get to.

2. *Leaders are perpetual learners.* And they encourage others to continue the search for improved knowledge.

3. *Leaders develop people.* They do it through role modeling, coaching, counseling, and mentoring. They try to give all birds in their environment the wings of eagles.

Leaders are people who give unselfishly to others, helping them achieve their goals and objectives. Is there a higher purpose?

Foundations of Achievement

As we build the foundation upon which *Habits of Wealth* rests, we need to take a look inside the achieving mind. First realize achievers are a highly diverse group. While focusing on achievement framed by entrepreneurial thought and behavior, we also acknowledge that not all achievers are entrepreneurs—and not all entrepreneurs are achievers. The definition of entrepreneur says nothing about achieving anything. Indeed, entrepreneurship requires only acceptance of the risk of a business or enterprise.

This book, then, is not about entrepreneurs. It's about achievers, many of whom mold their particular style of success around principles which are entrepreneurial. That makes them entrepreneurial achievers. It's when the two come together that magic occurs.

Here is a look inside an achiever's mind—a peek at some of the characteristics and habits forming the foundation of this book.

Entrepreneurial Achievers
Have Tremendous Desire

Achieving a significant, challenging goal is sometimes quite simple. The goal is so dominant little else matters. This level of hunger is a powerful, moving force that excites, motivates, and propels.

A burning desire manifests itself only when someone looks not at the challenge, but at the reward. Achievers with this kind of desire see the opportunity as fun. To them, the pleasure is in the journey, not the destination. An extraordinarily high belief in the value and worth of the goal anchors the intensity of one's desire to achieve. Significant achievers have an obsessive need, a dominating desire transcending ordinary thought.

Moving an idea or business out of the starting blocks is like the space shuttle leaving Cape Canaveral. The thrust required to clear the launch pad and travel the first 10 miles downrange is several times the power required for the remaining trip. Likewise, getting a business or idea off the ground requires its own form of thrust in the early going. Raw, gut-level desire provides the mental fuel to create this movement. Desire elevates the opportunity from a struggle, which is mere work, to a challenge, which provides entrepreneurial achievers with purpose and gratification.

Entrepreneurial Achievers
Are Highly Decisive

All the desire in the world is of little value without an accompanying decision to go for it, often in spite of considerable organizational or institutional resistance. As speaker Dave Yoho says, "The power of any idea is measured by the resistance it attracts."

Market research is a popular way to avoid a decision. It's used many times to defer a decision, rather than improve one. Insecure managers seeking to create maximum cushions for themselves point to market research if they're wrong—and take credit for the decision if they're right. A decisive achiever, however, always seeks to move things forward.

A second way to delay decisions is to form a committee. Unfortunately, committees seldom make significant decisions. Many committees exist not to *make* decisions, but to *avoid* them. And when they can't avoid them, the depersonalized decision relieves the participants of the risk of being wrong. Indecisive people tend to form committees—and belong to them. For obvious reasons, decisive achievers avoid committees when possible.

Effective decision-making is not a group function. Rather, ideal decisions come from one person, an individual tuned to opinion and consensus, but having the courage to stand up in the crowd and tell it like it is. And not look back.

The ability to make decisions and be comfortable with them is a primary characteristic of achievers. Thank God!

Entrepreneurial Achievers Have an Action Bias

Desire provides the fuel required to make decisions. The next step is the action phase—making something happen. It's action that creates results, and results create achievement.

Action means just what it implies: Recognizing an opportunity, then stepping out and giving a decision life. Achievers in the action phase are intensely interested in realizing the greatest return in the least time. While the achiever may often be impetuous in the action phase, that's more desirable than procrastination. The research is done. The ducks are in a row. Time to get down to business.

Those with a profound bias for action drive entrepreneurial America, and to some extent corporate America. They grease the wheels of enterprise, creating action where there was none. For them, the world of business is a field of luscious grass, and they've got the lawn mower.

Entrepreneurial Achievers Are Functionally Focused

Action requires not only that something get done, but that the right thing get done. Functional focus allows that to happen.

Highly focused individuals never begin a journey without reading a map. What good is it to travel 100 miles, only to find on arrival that you drove the wrong direction? Focus requires contemplation of the result, not just the process.

Functional focus usually occurs in a planned environment. An achiever working with a strategic plan has a much better shot at drawing a bead on his or her target and keeping it in sight—than someone without a written guide. Focus visits the organized mind. So it's no surprise that planning is a soulmate of the functionally focused individual.

Focused achievers know what they're *doing*. Functionally focused achievers, however, also know where they're *going* and burn the least amount of energy getting there.

Entrepreneurial Achievers Are Effective Risk-Takers

Entrepreneurs make their living *assuming the risk of a business or enterprise*. It follows, then, that risk-taking is a significant activity and that those who do it best are the real entrepreneurial achievers.

Although accepting risk is a continuing part of entrepreneurial life, it's not for everyone. Many prefer to "go with the flow." Avoiding a decision becomes a part-time job for them as they position themselves away from the battle. Not only do they not have to make decisions, they remove themselves from having to deal with any negative repercussions of those decisions. What a dull life!

"Don't exceed your comfort zone" is the first rule of risk-taking. As Harry Truman would say "If you can't stand the heat, stay out of the kitchen." There are many good, valuable people who are very uncomfortable with risk. That's OK.

Those who aren't risk-averse need to proceed with intelligence. As in decision-making, risk-taking is at its zenith when somewhat intuitive. But it needs support from objective information. A high risk might make sense when coupled with a very high potential reward. A low risk, however, is hardly appealing when married to a low reward. That's because functional focus allows one to develop only a limited number of ideas. And if you want to achieve something significant, those ideas must yield financial mileage. More often, moderate risk/moderate reward ideas emerge, and because they are the most often available, they're the entrepreneurial ideas most commonly implemented.

Entrepreneurial Achievers Are Inquisitive

One constant challenge of life is protecting ourselves from thinking we know enough. It's easy to become mentally lazy, although it seldom happens to outstanding achievers. They continue to barrel forward, turning the earth in search of information. And they gain it, at least in part, from other people. They practice one of the greatest of all skills—they ask questions. Asking a question is a way of learning more, preparing better, and adding value to personal relationships and decision-making skills. It's a way of asking for help. And it works.

Achievers, by definition, are looking toward the future, gaining new knowledge and developing an acquaintanceship with tomorrow. That new knowledge is the foundation of innovation and achievement.

An inquisitive mind is one of the achiever's most important assets. To be inquisitive is to be receptive to the opportunities and ideas of tomorrow.

Entrepreneurial Achievers Are Persistent

Persistence is powerful. An achiever can fall short in other areas and compensate for it with persistence. Persistence is to achievement what repetition is to learning.

Effective salespeople know most successes occur on the fourth or fifth call. If they quit after just two or three, they'll probably never make the sale. Regardless of talent, preparation, or product knowledge, a salesperson never achieves substantial success without persistence.

While critically important, persistence is a difficult characteristic to practice. The temptation to give up too soon is strong.

Like most sports, life is a game of inches, not feet or yards. Persistence plunges us forward. Many of the wealthiest, most successful achievers have reached their goals only after overcoming enormous obstacles and self-doubt.

Entrepreneurial Achievers Are Courageous

Courageous people are survivors. They zig when others zag. They say yes when others say no. They think in contrarian terms. They go against conventional wisdom. They set their own agenda and determine their own boundaries.

They also speak candidly. The courageous frequently say aloud what others only think about. It's not always easy or comfortable, but they do it because they have the inner need to "call 'em as they see 'em." We can't learn courage. We probably can't even develop it. Courage is an innate and instinctive application of what we believe is right or fair.

Entrepreneurial Achievers
Have, and Communicate, Vision

Several decades ago the Union Pacific was a major force in moving people by rail. How many people are they carrying today? We all know the answer. It's obvious they saw themselves in the railroad business. They weren't. They were in the transportation business. We should be taking Union Pacific Airlines on our business trips today. But there's no such carrier. They are a good example of what happens without vision. And that's why function-ally-focused vision is so important.

Being visionary requires that we ask ourselves important questions. Some of those questions come to the fore during planning. Others, such as "What business are we in?" are asked almost daily. Who knows what would have happened if Union Pacific would have asked themselves such questions a few decades ago.

I recently received a verbose, three-page letter from the CEO of a firm I've been doing business with for several years. A competitor put his company on the defensive when they made some effective strategic changes. He wrote the letter to explain what his organization was doing in response.

He said he was trying to *reposition* his company. The letter's purpose was to communicate his *vision* of that repositioning. Unfortunately, the long, meandering letter convinced me he had no idea what position he wanted to assume. The moral: When achievers communicate a vision, they do it in clear language and use as few words as possible. Extra words confuse rather than clarify.

Achieving remarkable feats requires we understand where we're going—and have the ability to communicate it.

Entrepreneurial Achievers Have Well-Defined Ethical Boundaries

Nothing is as important to my feeling of achievement as knowing it was accomplished ethically. Achieving at any cost is not the game I seek to win, nor one I want to play. To fight an entrepreneurial battle and emerge triumphant is only satisfying when the victory is untarnished. That requires not only outward respectability, but inward integrity.

Ethical issues surround us. Can you morally relate to being a marketing executive at a tobacco company, or its advertising agency, and spending your time finding ways to get people to smoke more cigarettes? We all arrive at intersections of life where ethical considerations must dominate. We can't let a transient need dominate a more permanent principle.

On occasion, we become involved in situations where our ethical standards are different from our peers'. What to do? Just do what you think is right. Our choice may bring temporary difficulty, but it will also bring long-term tranquility.

The word ethical has many synonyms—conscientious, decent, honest, humane, moral, noble, respectable, right, upright. Take your pick. The finest entrepreneurial achievers have these words in their vocabulary and their heart.

Entrepreneurial Achievers Invite Measurement

The achieving student looks forward to getting a report card; it's the same when we achieve professionally.

Workers periodically sit down with a supervisor to chat about how their jobs are going. Some see this as an opportunity, many don't. Why the difference? The answer lies in the individual's self-perception, how he or she comprehends his or her contribution. Those who just get by feel threatened by evaluation; those making a good effort welcome it. Attitude toward performance measurement parallels the individual conscience.

When you've put your all into a project or business, you see measurement not as a form of checking up but as an opportunity to show real colors. Achievers don't wait for others to keep score. They keep their own.

Entrepreneurial Achievers Have a Sense of Urgency

Here's a real opportunity for achievement. People with a sense of urgency get more done and do it on time. They create more positive and productive working environments; thus, the need for supervision decreases.

A sense of urgency drives an internal engine. The urgent doers are implementers. Once they latch onto an idea it moves forward through compulsive need to progress from thought to action, and from action to completion.

Entrepreneurial Achievers Understand Personal Limitations

There's a time to speed up and a time to slow down. Easier said than done.

Entrepreneurial maturity can be late in coming. We could paper entire offices with clippings from *Wall Street Journal* articles discussing mega-achievers with names like Trump and Campeau, Boesky and Milken. They didn't see their *slow* sign in time.

The entrepreneurial, achieving ego is both powerfully productive and potentially destructive. A sense of invincibility can set in after two or three successes. Instead of holding back some chips, the invincible achiever keeps letting them ride. More often than not it's because he or she is convinced he or she's so strong nothing can go wrong.

Strong, talented people often take their strengths too far. One of the valuable lessons of life is understanding when a personal strength, such as talent, becomes arrogance. That's when a wonderful asset becomes a destructive liability.

Entrepreneurial Achievers Control Fear

Fear is controlled, not overcome.

The dominant fear in professional life is the fear of failure. This anxiety blocks the path to the winner's circle for some. For others it creates total paralysis. The entrepreneurial achiever succeeds because he or she has at least partial control of the fear of failure.

Summary

These preceding foundations of achievement support the framework on which to build consistent, prolonged, and enlightened achievement. Any effort to achieve something outstanding constantly challenges the quality of our foundation.

The most frequent comment of the manuscript mentors I shared the following chapters with was "it will help people." You will find the information straightforward, uncomplicated, accessible, and fun. I hope when you finish you will agree it was helpful. May your achievements be many.

I

ACHIEVEMENT 101

---

*"A great pleasure in life is doing
what people say you cannot do."*
— *Walter Gagehot*

You are beginning a hands-on journey through 111 wealth-creating, achievement-oriented concepts and strategies you can take to the office tomorrow morning. *Habits of Wealth* will add to your skills and, perhaps more important, offer you and the people in your working environment a more fulfilling and rewarding professional life.

We have all taken prerequisite *101* courses in high school or college. That is what Chapter I is—prerequisite reading for achieving in an entrepreneurial decade.

ACHIEVING HABIT 1

Winning from the Beginning

"A winner is someone who sets goals, commits to those goals, and then pursues them with all available ability."

Setting a course toward entrepreneurial achievement is like commanding a ship. It may be the newest and mightiest in the fleet, but if it develops a faulty compass, even a seasoned commander will have difficulty getting it to the intended destination. IBM founder Tom Watson supported that belief. He pointed out IBM's success was no accident. Watson started IBM with a clear picture of what the company would look like when he was done.

Do your "compass check" early in your entrepreneurial journey. Imagine you're an Apollo astronaut racing to the moon. If you drift off course and make a correction during the first ten percent of the trip, your course adjustment is rather minor. If you wait until you are almost to the moon to make the adjustment, however, chances are you could not make the required correction before flying by and becoming another star in the galaxy.

The best sailors, pilots, and entrepreneurs have two things in common—they have a firm fix on their destination, and they make many small corrections early.

ACHIEVING HABIT 2

A Commitment
with Conditions

Achievement doesn't happen, it's caused. For some, commitment is a useless word. They can't use it because they don't have it. Achieving entrepreneurs must have commitment to a cause they believe in. Achievement requires it.

You have a choice of whether to be a *commitment avoider* or a *commitment exploiter*. Most achievers are deal-with-the-real, pragmatic people. They live in today's reality. Achievers commit to their dreams while under-achievers just dream. Will you accept dreaming as your contribution, or pay the price to commit?

The first condition necessary for commitment is belief—in your product or service. If you want to be an achieving salesperson, the product or service you're selling must conform to your ethical system. Otherwise, you won't commit. And if you don't commit, you won't achieve.

The second condition necessary for commitment is investment. The more you've thought, the more you've tinkered, the more money and time you've invested, the greater your commitment. There's a direct relationship between your level of investment and your level of commitment—and the enjoyment achievement provides.

The third condition necessary for commitment is ownership. The more personal the origin of an idea or the more unique and creative, the greater the importance it has to the creator and the easier commitment becomes. Lack of idea ownership is a major reason large organizations find it difficult to be entrepreneurial. An idea's identity is easily lost, and the resulting impersonalization dilutes the individual pride and enthusiasm necessary to sponsor an idea to completion.

Little is achieved without commitment. It creates growth and fosters self-esteem and self-determination. It gets us off "mental welfare."

You have a choice. What price are you willing to pay? Achievers have dreams. And they commit to them.

ACHIEVING HABIT 3

Quicksand Quotient I

Many entrepreneurs go into business seeking to build their net worth and, although they keep the doors open, wind up in financial quicksand.

Carefully examine your motivation *before* going into business. Are you looking for a job, or do you want to create wealth? Most new business ventures start to create a self-employment opportunity. That's okay. But if you're looking for a job, likely that's all you'll get.

The "job related start-up" increases the probability that you will become so involved in the business you and it will become synonymous. This common identity will dramatically reduce the value of the enterprise should you want to sell it. In fact, separating you from the business so you can sell it at any price will be a challenge. The moral of the story? Creating a job by going into business may get you nothing more than a decent living.

On the other hand, if your primary purpose is to create wealth, you need eventually to move away from running the whole show yourself. That requires the development of an effective team. Wealth is created by entrepreneurs who are willing, and sufficiently skilled, to build organizations. The business and the entrepreneur must be separable to build wealth.

ACHIEVING HABIT 4

Quicksand Quotient II

I participated in an ill-conceived start-up that had little chance to succeed. We were up against competition that was too dominant.

Hind sight is always 20/20! When considering development of a new business, be aware of the strength of the major player in the market. Regardless of the industry, if the market leader has more than 25 or 30 percent of the market, take a long, cautious look before proceeding. Competitors who already own large shares of the market dramatically reduce survival rates of newcomers. Odds are you will either run out of money trying to out-spend the big-hitter, or tire of the battle and back away. Even under optimum conditions, success will be an uphill fight.

To avoid quicksand when starting a business, determine:

1) Whether you're looking for a job or seeking to create wealth by building an organization that functions successfully without you.

2) Know the other players in the market. If one or more competitor is too dominant, watch out.

ACHIEVING HABIT 5

The Best Intuition Is Numerical Intuition

If you're like me, you remember a compliment for a long time. I'm still proud of one I received 15 years ago. An accountant doing the monthly books for one of my companies told me that I was the best *objective* accountant he knew. He was referring to my *knowing* the numbers on our profit and loss statement before seeing them—my numerical intuition.

Numbers are a road map, the primary way to determine whether or not you're on course. They're a way of knowing whether you are driving your company correctly, or whether you are too close to the ditch. Numbers are an achiever's second language, and one you must speak. Today's numbers become the basis for tomorrow's forecast. They represent what you expect to happen—your financial goals, your vision of the future.

Our staff accountant, Mike Peterson, plays a game with me every month. Before handing over the P&L, he asks me to estimate the month's profitability. I'm typically within five percent and often closer. An intuition for numbers separates goats from sheep. This important sixth sense allows the anticipation of important financial and other quantitative trends. Numerical intuition comes more naturally to some, but it's always a result of study, concentration, and experience.

To have a quality company you need quality numbers. Our staff has spent hours looking for a missing dime at monthly book closing—a discipline I highly recommend. When we publish our financial statements they are as correct as humanly possible. No *abouts* or *almosts*.

If your accounting statements aren't professional and accurate, they will lie. And when accounting lies, you are driving your business on a soft shoulder. Be sure your numbers are accurate. Get them quickly—within two weeks of month's end—and spend time with them. Learn your company's ratios and how one entry relates to another. It should become second nature.

Effective organizations have many common denominators. The emphasis put on the creation and understanding of correct financial numbers is crucial. Know your numbers. If you don't, your business is dead. Period.

ACHIEVING HABIT 6

Don't Just Know the Numbers, Know the Right Numbers

So you believe numbers are important. But what numbers? Sales, cost of goods, labor, and profit numbers get the most attention. But there is a number that doesn't appear on the P&L, yet it's more important than any that do. It's cash flow, the financial umbilical cord. Lack of growth does not cause all business failures. Some fail because they grow too fast. Failure, often caused by lack of cash, can occur even when the P&L shows an *acceptable* profit.

If you have a profit of $10,000 and accounts receivable increase $15,000, you lost $5,000 net cash, less depreciation. That's a profitable way to go broke.

Profit and cash are not the same. It's imperative we know what's happening to the cash account. Did it increase? Did it go down? How much is in the bank?

Here's a simplified monthly cash flow analysis format that provides an important overview of what's happening in the checkbook and how it can differ from reported profit.

SIMPLIFIED CASH FLOW ANALYSIS

NET INCOME (LOSS)	$15,000	This comes from the P&L statement.
Add: Depreciation	$1,500	A non-cash item from the P&L.
AVAILABLE CASH	$16,500	
Less: Debt Payments	$6,000	This is the principal portion of debt payments.
Dividends	$1,500	Paid out of retained earnings—doesn't appear on P&L.
Asset purchases	$4,000	This represents capital purchases such as equipment and improvements. Since these are depreciated they don't directly reduce profit.
Taxes-Fed/State	$3,500	This includes all income taxes paid, whether estimated or year-end.
TOTAL DEDUCTIONS	$15,000	
OPERATING CASH FLOW	$1,500	
REDUCTION OF RECEIVABLES (INCREASE)	($2,500)	Increase in receivables is a decrease in cash & vice versa.
FINAL CASH FLOW (LOSS)	($1,000)	

Bill Byrne

Summary

In this example, the profit statement indicates a profit of $15,000. The cash flow analysis, however, shows an operating cash flow of only $1,500, and a hard cash flow—after adjustment for increased accounts receivable—of a negative $1,000.

Is it possible to have a substantial *profit* and be broke at the same time? You bet.

Too many businesses look at profit, too few at cash flow. Your chances of staying in business, particularly in the first five years, dramatically improve if you pay more attention to cash flow than profit.

ACHIEVING HABIT 7

The Mathematics of Compounding Is Astounding

A day wasted or a decision delayed is expensive. Perhaps that's one of the reasons people who start early seldom lose their lead. Let's look at some examples of the mathematics of compounding:

You're 30 years old, and a company you founded currently earns $50,000 a year. What will it earn when you are 45 if earnings grow at a modest six percent a year?

Answer: $120,000.

What if everything above remained constant, except that earnings increased at 12 percent a year? Just double it to $240,000, right? Wrong.

Answer: $273,000.

Let's raise our sights. Your company now earns $100,000 annually. What will earnings be if you decide to retire in 15 years, given earnings growth of 10 percent a year?

Answer: $418,000.

Reaching even higher, the organization you founded nine years ago when you were 30 is earning $100,000 annually.

What will it earn when you're 60, assuming growth at a realistic 12 percent a year?

Answer: $1,080,000.

Bingo. A million dollars a year in earnings through the mathematics of compounding.

Money grows as a result of two forces—time and rate. Another reason to set your goals and get off the starting block early. Go get 'em!

ACHIEVING HABIT 8

A Lesson from the Mafia

Many successful entrepreneurs have a good understanding of the numbers, yet aren't numerically informed. Financial statements clouded with personal perks and extraordinary items don't reflect the organization's actual operating results or earning power.

Which leads us to our lesson from the mafia—keep two sets of books.

That may sound like an illegal proposal, but it isn't. One set of books should reflect financial performance from the perspective of an outsider interested in buying the company. I call it an *Operations Statement*. It excludes "owner transactions" and allows an uncontaminated look at true earning power—which is what a prospective buyer or appraiser needs to determine. Look at it this way: What expenses would an owner not employed in the business be able to do without? The owner's automotive expenses, life insurance premiums, dividends, owner compensation above what would be paid to someone assuming the owner's responsibilities, and unnecessary business travel are prime candidates. The other set of books may be the same as or very close to what you're doing now. The *Tax Statement* includes the above items and tracks your taxable income. It's an excellent tool for tax planning.

An Operations Statement removes extraneous items and shows an organization's real earning power—and earning power is what buyers pay for. Determine your company's value on the basis of the Operations Statement. It's useful for those on the outside, whether banker, potential buyer, or an appraiser placing a value on your business for financial planning.

ACHIEVING HABIT 9

Understanding Value Is a Valuable Understanding

Your ability to achieve is vested in providing a product or service that has perceived value. Note the word *perceived*. Effective marketing or positioning adds value which may exist only in the consumer's mind. These perceptions, however, are real. If the buyer thinks there's value, there's value.

Misconceptions exist as to what constitutes value. Most believe it's a function of price. If the price is low, there's more value than if the price is high. But price is only one component of value.

Value is actually a ratio of price to quality. Increasing price while keeping quality constant reduces value. Increasing quality with a constant price increases value. When both increase proportionally, value is constant. *Quality divided by price equals value.*

The most successful companies and products, those that have demonstrated the highest rates of growth and profitability over the long-term, are value-driven. The alternative, cost-driven, has a more volatile and less profitable history, perhaps because seller needs, not customer desires, determine pricing. When pricing your product, don't think cost. Think value.

ACHIEVING HABIT 10

Design It for Profit

"Quality is never an accident; it is always the result of high intention, sincere effort, intelligent direction and skillful execution; it represents the wise choice of many alternatives."

— *Willa A. Foster*

What is the relationship between product quality and profitability? The answer may surprise you. Various studies done in the '80s confirm that the most profitable companies over the medium- to long-term are those selling goods and services of high quality. Also, higher priced products yield a better return on sales and investment than lower priced products.

A high-quality product doesn't imply high-cost production. Many of our most efficient, profitable, and successful corporations combine a high-value product or service with low-cost production. That's a perfect combination.

Yes, organizations with the highest profits and profit margins are often achieving prosperity through quality. That's only part of the story. They're also constantly innovating and perfecting their niche strategy, habits critical in the development of the high-margin organization. High returns on investment and sales aren't accidental. High profitability is planned. Design your organization and your product for profitability.

ACHIEVING HABIT 11

Price It for Profit

"The worst crime against working people is a company which fails to operate at a profit."

Funny how many folks work so hard and don't bother to watch the bottom line. "Yeah, business is good, but I can't make any money at it," is what they sometimes say. I recently spent some time with a potential entrepreneur who had a dynamic concept and a darn good business plan. She's the type of person I hope makes it big with her idea. I'm glad we were able to talk about her proposed manufactured item because we focused on what I believe is a do or die decision for her—pricing.

It's possible she will be able to make her manufactured piece, sell it in quantity and pay herself a decent wage. But at her proposed price, that's the most she'll accomplish, and she'll need luck to do that. Her pricing thoughts provide virtually no chance for wealth creation.

That's just one of dozens of examples I could share on inadequate pricing. Entrepreneurs are often scared to death to price their product where appropriate profit margins are possible.

I've been in the restaurant business since 1973. On occasion, our peers have scorned us for our pricing. Yes it's true. Our prices have historically been slightly higher than other similar restaurants.

Unlike many, we actually practice effective pricing. We have constantly remained aware of the market, what our competitors are doing. We don't select a price because we're greedy. We're simply aware of what's going on around us and what we must do

---

to meet our Strategic Plan's goals for return on sales and investment, while providing perceived value to the customer.

For years I've observed businesses in many industries. I've rarely seen a company go out of business because it overpriced. On the flip side, I know several that have created overwhelming problems for themselves, including failure, because they didn't know what their costs were and had no idea what they needed to charge.

The most profitable organizations know where they are, both in internal needs and external environment. They have *pricing awareness*. Without it, owners become timid and unsure of themselves, creating a tendency to underprice.

Do you want a business that's a leader in its industry? Then become price-aware. Know the value of your product or service in the competitive marketplace. Match it to your needs, and price it for profit.

ACHIEVING HABIT 12

Don't Just Sell It, Collect for It

"Buy low, sell high, and collect early."

Meet the non-collector, probably a close relative of the low-pricer. To work hard and not make adequate profit is akin to selling hard without having an effective accounts receivable system.

If you have extraordinary sales ability or have attracted others to your organization who have, congratulations. You're a quantum leap ahead of much of your competition. Or are you? As spoils go to the victor, profit goes to the collector. Unfortunately, the large appetite of the highly productive salesperson usually doesn't extend into the collection phase.

If you have minimal collection problems with your customers, and I have large problems with mine, is it because you do business with all the good guys and I only the bad? I doubt it. More likely, you have a better receivables system.

Digging out of such a rut is much harder than avoiding it. Most businesses with a receivables problem aren't aware of it. You're a candidate for account receivables difficulty if:

1. You send both invoices and statements, creating confusion.

2. You intend to mail statements as close to the first of the month as possible, but "don't get around to it for a few days."

---

3. You don't have a *write-off* list that keeps you informed of what has been written off and for whom.

4. Your accounting system doesn't provide your financials to you routinely by the 15th of the month.

5. You continue to sell to accounts that are 60 or more days past due.

6. You don't post every payment every business day.

7. Your total receivables over 30 days exceed 15 days' average sales.

8. You don't employ a collection service for receivables over 120 days.

9. You don't produce a complete aging list by the 15th of the following month.

10. You don't have a standard procedure of communicating with late customers beginning no later than 75 days from initial billing.

To avoid or overcome a receivables problem, perform the ten items above ritualistically, plus:

1. Pay your sales staff a commission or incentive, but recapture it when an account reaches 60 days overdue.

2. When in difficulty, accelerate your receivables report from a 30 day interval to a 15 day interval.

3. Mail collection requests to overdue accounts in 15 day intervals.

4. There's nothing magic about billing only at the end of the month. You can also bill weekly or at time of sale if it makes sense.

Like many aspects of business, receivables problems often originate because of a lax attitude that *trained* the customer there was no hurry to pay. One of the necessary steps in cleaning up or avoiding payment problems is to change the customer's expectation. Make it known what your terms are and that you expect them followed.

Customers don't vary as much from business to business as receivables systems do. Accounts receivable problems are controllable, and when out of control, say more about the seller than the customer.

Slack accounts receivable management is a cancer that kills businesses. The remedy is internal organization and unfailing discipline.

ACHIEVING HABIT 13

Write It to Remember It

Forgetfulness, a plague to many and a concern of most, is a critical effectiveness robber. But there's a solution. It's a habit that increases productivity tremendously: *if it's worth remembering, it's worth writing down.*

Writing it down is also a stress remover, relieving the strain of trying to remember and freeing the mind to move on to other thoughts. Additionally, it avoids the feeling of guilt when something important is forgotten.

ACHIEVING HABIT 14

The Best Promotional Money You Won't Spend

Distribution of our magazine, the *Tri-State Neighbor*, covers a four state area. Our highly productive advertising and news staffs cover a lot of territory.

Our magazine has a fleet of silver station wagons. On the sides and back of each vehicle our logo is prominently and attractively displayed. Our effort is unique and creates a lot of comment and recognition. It has been a terrific tool, creating greater presence in our four-state coverage area. Our advertising manager says the high profile keeps her out of mischief—not one of our original intentions, but we take what we can get.

In 1989 our restaurant group introduced window paint to the upper Midwest, an inexpensive and, at that time, unique marketing tool. We believe it accounted for an immediate three percent sales increase. The increase paid for the signage in a couple of days, and it's still bringing them in!

Even though I'm in the media business, I know there are plenty of innovative ways to increase sales and profit without buying a second of air time or a column inch of ad space.

ACHIEVING HABIT 15

Timing Isn't Everything. Not Quite.

Question: You have a new idea. If your timing can't be perfect, is it better to be too early or too late? Achievers, who by their more aggressive and innovative nature reach the starting gate earlier than others, usually face a greater risk in being too early. Many suffer setbacks because they were too far ahead, and didn't have the financial staying power to wait for the market to develop.

Perhaps that's why many larger companies sit back and let others take the initial entrepreneurial risk. Unlike the entrepreneur, they have no reason to hurry, or so they think. They let others plant the tree. They watch it grow or die and move in only when life signs are thumbs up. It must be nice!

The superior idea does not always win. A well-timed product or service has a greater likelihood of success. Marketing the right idea into the right niche at the right time is an awesome combination. It's accomplished by an alert, savvy, and gutsy entrepreneurial achiever, perhaps with a little luck thrown in for good measure.

Bill Byrne

ACHIEVING HABIT 16

When Everyone Zigs . . . Zag

When I began the *Tri-State Neighbor*, a regional magazine for informed farm and ranch families in the depths of the farm depression in 1983, it was a bare bones start-up. I was a one-man show for the first nine months. My commitment and belief was high.

It worked. The magazine started strong and has moved at a gallop ever since. Ideally niched, it has provided valuable opportunities for our employees. It has also been effective for our customers, helping many of their businesses grow by redefining and broadening their geographical coverage. The regional concept of our magazine was totally new. We created and are effectively serving a unique regional trade area that allows advertisers to reach customers they couldn't efficiently reach before the introduction of our magazine. And it came to life during the worst cyclical downturn in agriculture since the '30s.

The *Tri-State Neighbor* is a classic example of contrary thinking. Agriculture was so depressed at the time that if I had gathered 100 people and told them of my idea, 99 of them surely would have told me I was crazy. In reality, only one person I shared the idea with thought it was a good one. His name is Frank Stinson, a highly successful auto dealer who taught me much about the power of regional marketing.

I remember a charity dance my wife, Lynne, and I attended between the time I decided to start the magazine, and when the first issue appeared. As is often the case, a friend asked what I was doing that was "new and exciting." I mentioned the concept of a regional magazine and shared my excitement for the idea. He caught my enthusiasm and asked why I thought it would work.

I recall answering, "Dick, I know it will. The market's waiting for it and I've done my homework." My "go against the cycle" intuition was yelling at me, and I went with it. I'm glad I did.

Bucking cycles is a profoundly important habit in building wealth, but it's not easy. Among those who do it poorly are managers and administrators who make their living concentrating on the business in front of them. Their close-in, internal focus isn't conducive to understanding the big picture.

On the other hand, entrepreneurial thinkers have an external focus, a higher awareness of the world about them. The entrepreneurial thinker isn't always smarter than the manager or administrator, just focused on more distant objects. External focus complements the entrepreneur's desire for change. The entrepreneur is thinking about creating another payroll while others are picking up their paychecks. This continual process of seeking change wears some down. If entrepreneurial leadership is present, however, change will occur. And change is at its best when it runs against a business cycle.

Contrary thinking is a powerful ally, helping one to lean into the wind while others are leaning with it. Contrarians buy stocks when others are complaining about the beating they're taking in the market. The contrarian startles the banker by wanting to borrow money to start a new business at the bottom of a recession. This is the same person who sells his stocks and his business to waiting buyers as the top of a cycle approaches. This is the person who is likely creating wealth. And he does it by zigging when others zag.

ACHIEVING HABIT 17

Don't Exceed Your Personal Speed Limit

"It's what you learn after you know it all that counts."

— *John Wooden*

The inflation of the early '80s made a lot of people look pretty smart. Our homes were worth more. So were farms and other real estate. Many segments of our economy came to believe they could borrow, borrow, borrow, and leverage, leverage, leverage. The rooster has come home.

Merv Griffin couldn't make payments on Resorts International, and it went into bankruptcy. Bill Farley acquired West Point-Pepperell at a price too high and defaulted. Robert Campeau paid too much for the Federated and Allied department store operations. And even The Donald (Trump) got fooled. The big boys aren't exempt. They are tumbling like dominos in a hurricane.

They all made the same mistake. They violated their personal speed limit. It happened when they convinced themselves that financial speed limits were for other people. Once again we're reminded capitalism has no favorites. We may have different size playing fields but we all use the same rule book. And it also shows the value of remembering one of my favorite adages: *Strength, when applied in excess, becomes a weakness.*

Just when we are certain that the stock market can only go up . . . it tumbles. Just when resort homes are so much in demand they can't fall in value . . . they plummet. Just when the bank thinks it's a good time in the business cycle to make a loan . . . they find they made the loan near the cyclical top. And just when world peace is a given . . . war breaks out.

Keep a wary eye on your speedometer. No one is exempt from the penalties for financial speeding. A hairpin corner is likely to appear just when you become certain the road ahead is flat and straight.

ACHIEVING HABIT 18

Luck Is No Accident

"The harder I work the luckier I get."
"Luck frequently visits the prepared mind."
"Luck is the residue of diligence."

Quotations about luck are everywhere. We all yearn for a streak of it, especially if it brings money.

Accidents do happen, but when luck is involved the lucky aren't selected at random. When Columbus courageously set sail in 1492 he was headed for the East Indies, not America. He got lucky. Ditto for Dr. Jonas Salk when he discovered the polio vaccine. What we refer to as luck results from *preparation and perspiration*. Idle, unprepared minds usually don't recognize opportunity. Neither will a negative mind that automatically goes into reverse when an innovative idea is proposed. The lucky pay their dues.

How can you get lucky? Here are a few thoughts:

1. *Be perpetually inquisitive.* Search for truth, for answers to questions important to you. Listen while others talk.

2. *Network.* Get out of your rut and meet new people doing new things and thinking new thoughts.

3. *Be positive.* Cheer for those who try.

4. *Diversify your interests.* Join Rotary, Kiwanis, or another service club to meet new and interesting people.

5. *Be willing to make mistakes.* They are necessary detours on the road to achievement.

6. *Maintain personal stability.* Unstable or volatile conditions eat up energy and distract from achievement.

7. *Be deserving.* Prepare for success. If you don't, it won't visit. If it does and you're not deserving, it won't stay.

8. *Treat people fairly.* They will appreciate it and may become an important future resource.

9. *Don't blame others.* Ultimately, your life is in your own hands. The blame game is for losers.

10. *Look for the edge.* Don't fall off, but try to find where it is and practice risk-taking in non-threatening ways.

11. *Develop role models.* Learn more about those who have achieved the goals you're still reaching for.

12. *Prepare your mind for success.* Achievement is like athletics. It requires preparation to win. Read aggessively.

ACHIEVING HABIT 19

Personally Yours

Clean, well-written, and personalized correspondence has tremendous value to both the entrepreneurial achiever and the organization. It's an area that deserves your priority attention. A few times a year I personally sign a batch of two or three hundred letters. Some would question the use of my time, but it's a priority that everyone in our organizations send professional, personalized letters. The people we're mailing to are important to us. They're worth whatever individual attention we can give them. I also sometimes write a note at the bottom of the letter if there's a personal thought or point of emphasis I want to share.

I'm proud I don't send letters out without my original signature. Even during an extended absence I have my administrative assistant forward correspondence to me for signing and mailing. It's also a matter of pride that my associates don't mail letters without their original signatures.

When you invest time to sign your correspondence, use an ink color other than black. The reader will know immediately that your letter is personal and that you care enough to sign his or her letter personally.

ACHIEVING HABIT 20

Professionally Yours

Sloppy letters give the sender a cheap, unprofessional image. I don't want letters making an impression I'm not proud of, so I don't send them if they're "almost OK."

As a dictator (of letters, thank you), I'm always fighting wordiness. Many of the poor letters I receive are dictated and not read. If you dictate, you or your secretary should make an effort to cut unnecessary words that creep into the recorder. If for some reason you can't read it before mailing, say so in the letter so the reader will better understand any imperfections.

Many people are wordy. Where did "enclosed please find" and similar trash come from? Write like you talk. Unnecessary words distract from your message.

An excellent quality check is simply to look at what you've written and take out the extra words. A letter with 20 words in two sentences is far more effective than saying the same thing in 40 or 60 words. Words are precious. Use them sparingly.

I often find myself deciding whether to send a typewritten letter, a handwritten note, or use the telephone. Most of the time I make my decision based on whether or not a written record is desirable. If so, it's typewritten. If not, I choose telephone or handwritten note, depending on the degree of formality. A note of caution—I've found myself writing personal notes too quickly, only to later discover I didn't convey the thoughts I intended. Proofread your handwritten notes, too.

ACHIEVING HABIT 21

Be a Risk-Taker, Not a Risk-Wisher

Entrepreneurship's dramatic growth is attracting those who want to be entrepreneurs but shouldn't be—the dreamers who spend their lives climbing on the bandwagon. They're not risk-takers, they're risk-wishers. How do we tell one from the other?

It's easy. A risk-wisher merely "goes with the flow," while the risk-taker creates the flow through preparation. Good risk-taking requires preparation. Risk-taking without preparation is gambling. And that's not the business the entrepreneurial achiever is in.

I started my first business, a franchised restaurant, at age 28. My preparation began at 19 when I started reading every piece of franchise information I could get my hands on. I prepared for nine years before making an investment in the franchising concept. While I'm not suggesting everyone needs nine years to make an effective decision, I am suggesting that successful risk-taking is a planned process. It's foolish to put your money down before your homework's done.

The unprepared risk-wishers are less likely to achieve for a second reason. They are too sensitive to what others think and therefore will be more inclined to enter a business that projects a desired *image*. When you make an investment, especially your first one, don't try to impress others. Try to impress your pocketbook.

Getting a good start on your new business requires more than an investment of money. It requires an investment in knowledge and preparation. To do it any other way isn't risk-taking. It's risk-wishing. And it doesn't work.

ACHIEVING HABIT 22

What to Look for in a Banker

A serious entrepreneur is constantly in the process of evaluating new opportunities. Therefore, capital is an ever-present need. The selection of a good bank is paramount to future success. If you want a lot of mail, send a questionnaire to entrepreneurs asking them to grade their bank and make suggestions for improvement.

An adversarial relationship frequently exists between bankers and entrepreneurs. The entrepreneur sees the banker as a stuff-shirted, non-risking person with a big desk and no guts. The banker, on the other hand, has seen too many inexperienced, pie-in-the-sky hopefuls who don't know a business plan from a frying pan.

Many years ago someone told me, only partially in jest, that a bank was a good place to get money if you didn't need it. While that perspective is "on the money," it is unfair to the many bankers who have supported entrepreneurs (this one included) when they believed in the person and the idea.

Building a solid relationship with a bank is possible, even in the initial phase. But don't establish a relationship with just any bank. You want the best. Your choice is crucial to your success.

Terry Schulte is one of the most successful new car dealers in the Midwest. While discussing employee turnover, I asked him about the stability of his automotive sales force. His answer was, "My goal is to have a lower level of turnover at my dealership than my bank has among the loan officers it assigns to me."

Loan officer turnover is an important consideration. Twenty years ago I began a commercial banking relationship, and my loan officer is still with the same bank in the same town. He understands me and I understand him. Our relationship's continuity has been critically important to my achievement. He once told me that when I wanted to do something badly enough I would get it done. His opportunity to watch me, and me him, has been a mutual benefit. Find out about the bank's loan officer turnover. If it's high, go somewhere else.

When looking for a banking partner, prepare to ask pertinent questions. The answers will not only provide valuable information, they will also serve to let the banker know you've done your homework and take this decision seriously.

You don't want the bank to interview you. Remember—you're the customer. Interview the banker. View the bank as a potential supplier, in this case of money and financial services.

Here are some questions every serious entrepreneur should ask a potential banker:

1. *What do you know about my business?* Educating them is not your job.

2. *What experiences have you had with entrepreneurs?* Listen closely. You should learn both the scope and quality of their experience and how that has molded their current attitude toward entrepreneurs.

3. *Tell me about the entrepreneurs you have on your Board of Directors?* You'll probably hear the names of corporate presidents who control large deposits. However, if they speak of two or three entrepreneurial achievers they helped in their initial years, you have a clue that you may be important to them. Banks who seriously want to cultivate business with entrepreneurial thinkers find ways to interact with them, to learn from their side of the fence. Board membership is one way entrepreneurial banks accomplish this.

4. *Who makes your loan decisions?* The closer the decisions are made to the customer, the better. If it's a chain bank and too many decisions are made at the regional or national office, forget it. They won't be able or willing to factor in the quality of the individual. Both their loan decisions and your relationship with them will be impersonal. You'll get lost.

5. *How long do loan decisions take?* Banks sometimes take three weeks to make decisions that need only three days—or three hours. Learn about their decision-making process. Ask about the dollar limits on local decisions. Entrepreneurs are somewhat impatient while banks are committee-oriented. This varying sense of urgency can cause conflict. Deal with it early.

6. *Have you had any difficulties with your bank examiners in the last five years?* This might appear an unusual question, but it's highly pertinent. When regulators get nervous, the bank does, too. It impacts the customer. The bank re-evaluates customer credits, loan parameters can suddenly change, and the bank may accelerate the frequency of their requests for financial statements. Avoid a bank with these problems, or their problems will become yours.

7. *How frequently do you require financial statements, and what do you want to see?* Your bank has every right to monitor your business closely, perhaps quarterly for the first year or two, or longer if there are serious concerns. However, the requirements for successful businesses should drop to semi-annually or annually under most conditions. American enterprise is shortsighted, an ailment caused in part by shortsighted banking policies. Successful businesses need flexibility to play out their vision without someone looking over their shoulders wondering how profits look this month.

8. *Inquire about their credit-scoring software.* Spread sheets now analyze customers. Most banks will share information on their particular methods so you can gain knowledge of

what financial information they look at and its degree of importance.

9. *Understand their service charges.* Bank service charges are increasing, but not all banks are increasing them at the same rate. Compare the charges from bank to bank and understand why they require them. This alone could save you tens of thousands of dollars over time.

Bankers have a habit entrepreneurial achievers should be aware of. Every individual and institution has two methods of decision making—rationally and emotionally. Observing banker's habits convinced me of one absolute: they're highly emotional lenders. It's a habit anyone growing a business should be aware of.

Almost everything has a cycle, be it a business, a marriage, interest rates, or the economy. An expansion has followed every recession in history. Every one! And at least a slight recession follows every expansion. Which begs the question: Why do banks insist on opening the lending faucets toward the top of the business cycle and closing them at the bottom? Because they're emotional.

The August 24, 1990, edition of the *Wall Street Journal* discussed banking industry emotionalism. The article concerned a real estate credit squeeze in Nashville. John Clay, CEO of Nashville's Third National Bank, didn't minimize the real estate debacle or the role area banks played in it when he said, "The banks have been running all over each other to make deals. It's time to pay the piper." Another Nashville bank official, Neil Cunningham of First American Corporation, said there was "an unspoken wave of caution" pervading his bank. "You're dealing with human emotion," Cunningham concluded.

I was raised as the eldest of six children on an Iowa farm, an area that has some of America's prime farmland. The value of an acre of land at the cyclical peak in 1980 was about $3,500. Five years later the value of the same acre was less than $1,200.

If, at the 1980 peak, the farm I grew up on had sold at $3,500 an acre, virtually every banker in the county would have chased the buyer down Main Street to make the loan. Yet had the farm sold five years later to the same buyer at the cyclical bottom of $1,200, every bank in the county would have been highly skeptical of the loan and buyer financing would have been difficult to obtain. Same land. Same buyer. Yet financing becomes more difficult at $1,200 an acre than at $3,500. Pretty ridiculous, but true. And it's because bankers too often feel with their emotions rather than think with their brain. In this example, they were wrong twice.

You will benefit from understanding this unique banking mentality when looking for credit. The scarcity of funds at the bottom of an economic cycle makes development or expansion of a business even more frustrating for someone who understands cyclicality and wants to invest at the bottom.

If bankers would adopt Wall Street's buy low, sell high theory they would make more money. So would their customers. And both bankers and borrowers would get into less trouble.

ACHIEVING HABIT 23

What a Banker Wants to See in You

A good banking relationship serves both the bank and the customer. To the bank, a credit request is an opportunity. If it doesn't loan to its profit-maximizing potential it will lose earnings (business customers pay higher interest than the bank's principal investment alternative, government securities).

The bank's primary need is to be repaid, and the customer's opportunity is to meet that need. How can you convince a bank that you'll pay the loan back? Be professional, prepared, and truly informed about the industry or niche you wish to enter. Keep in mind you are dealing with people in an industry that has an emotional bias. That opens another avenue to success: Psychology.

I'm certainly not trying to diminish the seriousness of developing a valuable, lasting relationship with a bank by discussing it in a psychological context. What I do seek to emphasize is that bankers sometimes make decisions based on both financial and non-financial considerations. To get a banker's attention, equip yourself with all the knowledge and savvy possible.

Put on your best face by conducting yourself in a way that disguises your need for credit. Money is more difficult to get when you need it, so if you come across as if you don't need it, a banker is more likely to give it to you. Your odds improve when you appear unemotional, businesslike, and fully able to survive with or without the bank's money.

Every bank is a good bank when you don't need one. Determine the value of a banking relationship during your important and sometimes difficult entrepreneurial crossroads. If your bank is there when you need it most, it deserves your highest loyalty. Give it. If it's not there when you need it, or if they change the rules frequently, go somewhere else.

When you join forces with your banker don't betray his or her confidence. Be a responsible and responsive communicator. Update your banker regularly, not just when the news is good. Build confidence that, above all, you're a good communicator and a person of honesty and integrity.

Several successful years down the road you may wish to develop a secondary banking relationship. Bankers are interested in new business, and it won't hurt a bit to hatch some of your eggs in a new basket. Remember, bankers are emotional, so creating a little competition often works well.

ACHIEVING HABIT 24

Inside the Achieving Personality

Outwardly, achievers look much like everyone else. Inwardly, there's a difference. They hear their own tune and play it on their own instrument. Achieving people share many common denominators, and although present in widely varying intensities, these similarities provide an opportunity to construct a highly reliable profile of the instincts and habits of an achieving personality.

The *typical* achiever is likely to be:

Impatient.

Excessive in some habits, both personal and professional.

Highly self-confident.

Committed to the task, often showing tendencies toward thinkaholism, sometimes toward workaholism.

A highly responsive problem-solver.

Very pragmatic and honest with self and others.

Intensely interested in exploring new knowledge.

In control of own environment.

Impact driven.

Particular as to likes and dislikes.

More introverted than extroverted.

Highly self-sufficient.

More interested in being respected than being liked.

Unusually forthcoming and direct.

Turned off by failure, but understands it's a piece of the achievement puzzle.

A good salesperson when accompanied by strong belief and passion.

Exceptionally goal-oriented.

A corporate dropout.

Disinclined to delegate.

Attracted to challenge.

Aware of obligations to others.

Attracted to both highly entrepreneurial and highly non-entrepreneurial environments, and less attracted to those in between.

A heavy reader of non-fiction.

Very resourceful, especially in the face of adversity.

An effective contingency thinker.

Precise in expectations of self and others.

Demanding but fair.

Highly project-focused.

Mentally organized.

Willing to mentor.

Firm and opinionated, not often in a gray area.

Reliable and predictable.

Contemplative of the future and its potential.

II

FRANCHISING: THE ENTREPRENEURIAL OPPORTUNITY OF THE NINETIES

"Franchising is the business phenomenon of the last quarter of this century."

Starting a business is serious business. Many don't take it seriously enough.

The Small Business Administration (SBA) says that 63 percent of new businesses fail within the first six years. Even among the businesses that stay open, only three percent are ever strong enough to reach one million dollars in sales. These statistics are telling. If you're average, the odds are only three in eight that your new business will survive six years. And even among the survivors, reaching the million dollar revenue mark happens only one time in 12.

Being an entrepreneur can be a gut-wrenching experience. In addition to meeting the emotional demands, entrepreneurial success requires courage, commitment, and a positive, assertive I-can-do-it-in-spite-of attitude. And an idea.

The idea is only the beginning. Taken by itself, an idea is worthless, as shown by the many people we meet who have a good idea and fail to develop it. Ideas are dormant until teamed with an entrepreneurial mind.

Enter the franchisor with a business opportunity. Unlike 99 percent of the other ideas, something is being done with this one. The franchisor brings a concept the entrepreneur can bite in to and evaluate.

When someone franchises an idea it indicates the spade work is complete to move an otherwise lifeless, unsponsored concept to the level of opportunity. Is buying a franchised business for you, and you for it? The franchised format provides a vantage point to make an entrepreneurial decision. And make it more accurately.

The prospective franchisee must ask many questions. How much money will we need? Who will be our customers? What's unique about this product or service that will entice the consumer? Is there a niche? Will it be large enough? What will the margins be? Will they meet our needs and goals? How fast is the market growing? How long will it take to break even, etc.?

One of the major benefits of franchising is its ability to change an inert, valueless idea into a living opportunity. No longer a mental abstraction, but an assessable opportunity. There's something to act on. Franchising is like a good pair of glasses, allowing quicker and more accurate recognition of entrepreneurial opportunities.

FRANCHISING
HABIT 1

Franchising Defined

Thinking about buying a franchise? You're not alone. Two words currently describe franchising: growing and thriving.

John Naisbitt, author of *Megatrends*, calls franchising "the single most successful marketing concept ever." Its dramatic growth continues. Its competitive edge is documented.

Franchising is a business method, a system of selling goods and services. A franchise exists when:

1) The use of a trademark is authorized.

2) There's an ongoing relationship between a franchising company and a franchised business owner.

The Franchising Success Story

Why is the franchise system succeeding? The answer lies in the important advantages it offers both a company wanting to finance its growth and the entrepreneur looking for opportunity.

From your perspective, you want to invest your capital in yourself. You're confident you can make it but want a safety net to reduce risk. You have read about the success of many franchises and probably have a friend or neighbor who is a highly successful franchisee. How could you better capture the ready asset of trademark identification, capitalize on the accumulated experience of others, and buy into advantages such as advertising assistance and proven operating systems?

From the franchisor perspective, franchising is a provider of external capital. There is no need to go deeply into debt or give up a large part of the company to a venture capitalist, and the system will potentially grow much faster. Also significant is the opportunity to attract talented, often experienced franchisees, thereby positively leveraging both the quality and quantity of future growth.

The prospective franchisee has another important advantage—the self-policing effort of the International Franchise Association. IFA members have agreed to a Code of Ethics providing for full disclosure and accuracy of all materials they distribute. Be sure your potential franchising partner is an IFA member.

When the franchisor and entrepreneurial franchisee join forces it creates the best of all possibilities. The entrepreneur benefits from the market-proven opportunity, and the franchisor attracts the capital for expansion and the talent for success.

Franchising can provide a firm foundation for a fertile future. Every entrepreneur looking to expand business horizons should examine this method closely.

FRANCHISING
HABIT 2

The Nineties: The Decade of Franchising

The bright outlook for franchised entrepreneurship isn't accidental. The International Franchise Association estimates that 90 percent of these businesses succeed. Contrast this with the SBA report showing 63 percent of non-franchised businesses failing in their first six years. No wonder franchising is becoming the business form of preference. And no wonder franchising and entrepreneurs have become fast friends.

Franchising simplifies. One ongoing challenge of the entrepreneurial mind is finding societal needs to profitably fill. The franchise format turnkeys that for the entrepreneur, allowing the franchised business to start not with the difficult need-defining phase, but with the less intimidating task of offering the consumer a proven solution.

The franchisee's ability to bypass the need-defining phase is significant, as the high rate of non-franchised business failures identifies closely with this initial level of entrepreneurial activity. Need-defining is to a solution as creativity is to innovation. As Harvard professor Theodore Levitt put it, the difference between creativity and innovation is the difference between thinking about getting things done and getting things done. Having the initial need-defining creativity done, and in a way that confirms its accuracy, is one of the reasons entrepreneurs are flocking to buy franchises.

Franchised businesses generated 39 percent of the retail sales in the U.S. in 1991. By the turn of the century, authorities expect those sales to top 50 percent. Imagine—a business concept generating more than half our country's retail sales. No other business method comes close to having such an impact on our economy.

FRANCHISING
HABIT 3

Who's Buying What and Why?

The typical buyer of a franchise isn't typical anymore. The demographics are moving upscale. A recent joint study by DePaul University and the franchise consulting firm, Francorp, Inc. of Chicago, concludes that new franchisees have money, education, and business experience.

For example, the study shows 35 percent of new franchisees are professionals with management experience, 30 percent are non-supervisory white collar workers, and 15 percent are blue-collar workers. Additionally, more than 40 percent have a bachelor's degree. The franchise buyer's average income is $67,000, with 25 percent making over $75,000.

Virtually every conceivable product and service will become available in the franchised format this decade. Look for medical services, general construction, plus various services targeted to help the working mother. Other fast-growing segments include training services, employee leasing firms, and businesses dealing with health and personal appearance.

While this industry has been relatively immune to business cycles, that could change. With so much growth ahead, a new franchisee will need to be cautious that the business niche chosen has sufficient product or identity differentiation.

FRANCHISING HABIT 4

How to Evaluate a Franchise

Yes, franchise locations are increasing dramatically. Yes, franchising will be a strong growth area this decade. But no, franchising is not for everyone.

Not all are of equal quality. Like other entrepreneurial opportunities, franchising can be a gold mine—or a mine field.

Complete a thorough "due diligence" before investing in such a business. Here's a partial pre-investment checklist:

1. *Develop an understanding of the geographic regions where the franchise operates.* One risk of expansion is moving the concept into regions where lifestyles or ethnic composition may be different from areas where the franchise now operates. Not all franchise concepts adapt profitably to every part of the country.

2. *Ask for volume information by region.* This will improve your understanding of any "regional revenue bias" that may exist.

3. *Seek information on volume by year location opened.* You'll learn what volumes new locations experience—especially important to early cash flow analysis. An understanding of volume levels in two-, five-, and 10-year-old installations will also be useful in predicting success.

4. *Ask the franchisor to provide, for the last three to five years, the number of locations operating at the end of each fiscal period.*

5. *Seek opening and closing data for the last three fiscal years.* This takes your inquiry beyond the number of locations operating. For example, a franchisor may show it had 100 locations open at the end of the last fiscal year. One year later, it has 110 operating. Did they open 10 franchises? Not necessarily. They may have opened 20 and closed 10. There's a big difference.

6. *How many locations does the franchisor operate?* Usually, but not always, the best franchising opportunities exist where the franchisor operates at least 10 percent of total locations. This number is often 20 or 30 percent. This is a good indicator of their operating knowledge, their belief level, their financial capacity, and their management depth.

7. *How successful are the company-owned locations?* You will garner critical information here. Ideally, company-owned locations should be showcases for the franchise. Visit them. If they're not up to your ideals you may want to scratch this company from your prime list. The best franchisors lead their system. You should be concerned if you don't find such leadership.

8. *How many locations has the franchisor bought from franchisees?* If the franchise is more than 10 years old the answer you want is "yes, some were purchased." If none have been, determine whether they're in a financial position to purchase, should the opportunity present itself. The franchisor's ability to purchase is critical for several reasons.

    One of the most important surfaces when a major franchisee wants to sell. The integrity of the system is solidified when the franchisor's position is that of a potential buyer—if only to provide assurance that this large, important operation doesn't fall into the wrong hands.

    Top franchising companies occasionally buy out their larger and stronger franchisees. There are reasons. It provides stability to the system and prevents the franchisee from going out on his or her own, a temptation for larger and more sophisticated operators. It also benefits the morale of smaller operators, motivating them to grow and prosper because the acquisition gives them a vision of the wealth that success may bring.

A franchisor with financial strength and operational credibility is an important asset. The last concern a franchisee needs is for a nearby operator to run a business outside of franchise requirements, and not have a franchisor strong enough to deal with the problem.

As AT&T used to say, "the system is the solution." Maintaining conformity of product, service, and image within the system is what you're paying for. Find a franchisor with the financial and management teeth to provide it.

9. *Discuss market penetration within the Area of Dominant Influence (ADI).* Site selection needs are changing dramatically. The most successful franchise entrepreneurs, now and into the early part of the 21st Century, will organize their businesses with marketing economies and management efficiency foremost in mind.

For example, if you're entering the retail food industry, an important inquiry relates to how many locations the franchisor has within the ADI—a term referring to the geographic area served by dominant radio and television signals. If you're the only one around, you may not be able to afford the high media costs required for success.

On the other hand, if there are already many operating locations within your ADI you can cooperatively pool your funds and have immediate media muscle. It is especially beneficial to have a large and successful franchisee operator in your ADI to provide marketing leadership and an opportunity to network on your road to success.

Promotional clout and managerial efficiency are critical to achievement in franchising. Have a plan that provides you both.

10. *Gather complete financial information.* Franchising has full-disclosure requirements, but seldom does that include examples of profitability. Franchisors will play this down, but be persistent in securing pro-forma financial statements. Only the persistent get financial information adequate to make a good decision. Be particularly sensitive to return on sales (ROS) and return on investment (ROI).

11. *Talk to other franchisees.* Important information and a good perspective may come from existing operators. Don't sign up without it.

FRANCHISING
HABIT 5

Financing Your Franchise

Franchising's prosperity is remarkable. It has flourished in spite of, not because of, traditional lenders. Twenty years ago, if a franchisor wanted to sell a franchise, the franchisor's banker often provided the funds. This allowed the franchisor to make the sale and grow the system. The franchising industry is indebted to these pioneers who accepted much of the risk of building the franchising concept from the ground up.

Until recently, the local bank hasn't been the place for a prospective franchisee to look for money. That is slowly changing. Banks traditionally loan on assets. That clashes with one of the strengths of franchising, since they are typically low asset enterprises. The bank wants assets, the franchisee figures he's better off not having to buy them. Consequently, the franchisee doesn't have assets to collateralize, and the bank loses interest. It's a vicious circle.

The situation is improving for many good reasons. First, bankers are increasingly aware the failure rate of franchised businesses is significantly lower than non-franchised ones. Second, banking is shifting toward cash flow lending, a strong area of most franchised businesses. And third, franchising is attracting better educated, more experienced people. Such changes are accelerated by many positive banking relationships built over the years by successful, pioneering franchise operators. These operators have provided bankers insight into the wealth-creating potential of franchised businesses.

Bankers are developing larger appetites for franchise financing. Some of the larger lenders are even creating new departments to serve franchise customers. Therefore, your local banker may now be more inclined to talk seriously with you.

FRANCHISING
HABIT 6

The Dollar Deception

Business writers use too much ink talking about the importance of capital to business startup. In most cases an organized, thoughtfully-developed opportunity presented by a knowledgeable and prepared entrepreneur will find money. It may not be easy, but winning opportunities get money.

Most successful businesses start with inadequate capital. Contrary to popular belief, having plenty of money often creates more problems than it solves. Having little concern about the checkbook promotes waste and sloppiness. It creates inefficiencies the organization may never get rid of. In addition, adequate funding may allow the company to get overly ambitious too fast.

My experience shows tight initial capital serves the beginning entrepreneur well. Most organizations that become high achievers start small, keep it simple, and run a tight ship. The lessons learned early in the entrepreneurial process are not only remembered the longest but are the most valuable. Having to be cautious with a dollar is the most important lesson of all.

FRANCHISING HABIT 7

Franchising's Top Five Start-Up Priorities

We need dozens of ingredients stirred together when starting an achieving, successful franchised business. Here's a brief description of the five I believe to be most important:

First Priority: *Form a capable team.* There's no substitute for talent. Strong aptitude applied to a mediocre opportunity can produce outstanding results. On the other hand, weak aptitude applied to a fantastic opportunity is likely to produce only moderate results.

With talent you can achieve almost anything. Without it you will achieve much less. Hire it. Admire it. And keep it.

Second Priority: *Get the location right.* "How do they sell so much of that stuff at those prices?" We've all heard these words of amazement. More often than not, it's because the business is well-located.

A good location isn't a necessity for all franchised businesses. If you're in retail, however, heed the oft-used cliche: The three most important ingredients of success are location, location, location. It's usually true.

Third Priority: *Select a quality franchisor.* You needn't be a rocket scientist to learn that the quality of franchisors runs the gamut—from inept to extraordinary. There's a tendency to think the abilities of the franchisor won't make much difference. After all, you're in business for yourself. Not true. Many franchisors have hampered the growth of their franchisees by inadequate investment in their business or lack of business sophistication.

It's not uncommon for successful franchisees to surpass the skills of the franchisor in many areas. When this happens, the franchisee begins to wonder what he or she is paying for. These people become apprehensive about making additional investment in their franchise and often go elsewhere.

The (franchisee) tail wags the (franchisor) dog in many situations. That's bad news. Choose a franchisor capable of aggressive market leadership, then hop on for the ride.

Fourth Priority: *Have a numbers person.* Many entrepreneurs suffer from *numnorance*, the ignorance of numbers. Every achieving organization has at least one good numbers person. Numnorance and entrepreneurial achievers are like oil and water. You seldom find them together.

Fifth Priority: *Choose your industry carefully.* Capital and success travel in the same crowd. Lenders court some industries and shun others. Be sensitive to the reputation of the industry you're considering. Financing often depends more on lender perception of the industry than the individual's reputation.

FRANCHISING
HABIT 8

Why Franchisees Fail

Franchised businesses fail for many of the same reasons non-franchised ones do, just not as often. I have carefully studied faltering and underachieving businesses for years, and the reasons they don't live up to their potential repeat themselves over and over. Here are the top dozen:

1. Unsophisticated franchisor.
2. Undercapitalized franchisor.
3. Ineffective key employees.
4. Weak employee incentive compensation programs.
5. Inadequate business plans.
6. Wrong site selection.
7. Inadequate market testing.
8. Poor accounts receivable techniques.
9. Significant forecasting errors.
10. Lack of niche development.
11. Weak marketing.
12. Improper pricing.

FRANCHISING HABIT 9

Checklist for Buying an Existing Franchised Business

Perhaps you'll buy an existing franchised business rather than start one. Although many of the decisions are the same for both, there are also dissimilarities. No list is complete for all situations. Look at this checklist and expand it as appropriate:

General Examination

1. Review the franchise agreements thoroughly. Determine under what conditions the franchise rights are transferrable. Also check the time left on the franchise agreement and the franchisor's intention to renew.

2. Determine whether equipment is owned or leased. Check all equipment warranties and maintenance agreements.

3. Check property leases for changeover fees assessed when new lessee assumes lease.

4. Ask a professional to place a value on goodwill, usually valued between zero and 2.5 times annual pre-tax profit.

5. Assess future potential in the context of whether or not to buy the business, not how much you should pay for it.

Financial Examination

1. Analyze financial statements for the last three to five years. Focus your analysis on cash flow.

2. Check tax returns for the past three to five years.

3. Review the previous four quarterly sales tax and payroll tax returns.

4. Examine pension and profit-sharing plan reports for the last two years.

5. Obtain a list of all employees showing names, length of employment, position and responsibilities, how compensated, earnings history for last three years, stock ownership, and potential for retention.

6. Examine detailed depreciation schedules.

7. Compile an asset list including land, buildings, furniture, and equipment. Determine acquisition date, cost, estimated current market value, depreciated value, condition, remaining useful life, and current appraisal.

8. Review receivables and payables procedures, receivable aging procedures, and present receivables status.

9. Reconcile the seller's inventory claims with your own.

10. Compile a list of debt and lease payments and determine debt service requirements.

11. Detail all liens, collateralized assets, judgments, past due accounts, and supporting documents.

12. Determine that the financial relationship with the franchisor is current.

Buying a business, whether franchised or not, can be tricky. Remember, there's a reason it's for sale. Be thorough, and *caveat emptor*.

FRANCHISING HABIT 10

The Strong Case for Market Penetration

Larry Manning was a franchisee in Texas. He was a good businessman in most respects and considered a potential star by the franchisor.

Larry's many talents included being an excellent pilot. He flew at every opportunity, even flying to destinations more suited to driving.

Over several years Larry developed more than a dozen franchised restaurant locations in Texas. Everything went well for awhile. Then the restaurant business became more competitive. His restaurant group collapsed and the bank repossessed his plane.

One error caused Larry Manning's failure. Even though he had twelve restaurants, they were spread over seven Texas communities. That's fine for a pilot on a pleasure trip, but not for an entrepreneur trying to make a living.

The successful franchisers of the '90s will develop dominance in their geographic areas. Market penetration requires a concentration of locations within a defined ADI marketing area, allowing the creation of maximum consumer awareness and operating efficiency.

Few philosophies of success are as important to the franchising community as market penetration. It's amazing that so many franchisors have led franchisees down the road of ruin by neither practicing nor understanding the role of market penetration in success.

The value of penetrating one's market is shown by its impact on two increasingly important overhead components—management and media.

Think big when you start. That may lead you to open your franchise in a market that accommodates growth. View your new business as a cluster of multiple locations under the protection of a single umbrella. Under that umbrella is your management team and all the advertising mediums you will use. Thus, the team and the media are able to cover your entire cluster of locations effectively.

Larry Manning would likely be financially healthy today if he had been less interested in being a hot-shot pilot and more interested in pursuing dominance in one or more select markets.

Management and media—two arenas where the battle for the consumer's business will take place. Organize your future to fight the battle efficiently.

FRANCHISING
HABIT 11

Effectiveness and Efficiency: Cousins, but Not Blood Brothers

"An efficient businessman who found a machine that would do half his work bought two."

Franchising is a proven business method. Efficiency is one important reason for its substantial success. As a business strategy, it is highly productive, operable, and functional. It eliminates the need to reinvent the wheel for every start-up. It reduces the stumbling in the early stages. It produces quicker results with reduced movement. Clearly, it's an *efficient* system of doing business. But it's not *effective*.

We often think the two words are interchangeable. They're not. People are effective. Systems, such as franchising, are efficient. The efficiency of franchising helps the franchisee be effective.

Think of franchising as a form of priority management which requires concentration of effort on doing the right thing. Someone who manages priorities effectively manages time effectively. People are effective. Systems are efficient.

Bill Byrne

FRANCHISING
HABIT 12

Working Together: The Franchisor and the Entrepreneurial Franchisee

Franchising attracts many creative and innovative people. But it requires uniformity. Sound like trouble? Indeed, it seems franchisors and entrepreneurs make strange bedfellows. Yet successful franchisees are highly entrepreneurial. Earlier in the chapter I noted the difference between creativity and innovation. Therein lies the potential for our strange bedfellows to sleep peacefully.

Creativity is the process of defining new problems, while innovation is applying new solutions to an already identified problem.

Let's say you want to buy a franchise. To do so requires comfort with the franchisor's creative, problem-defining decisions. You like what you see. You become a franchisee, and with the creative process already completed, you merely read the manual, become a robot, and live happily ever after. Interested?

Of course not. And that's not how franchising works. While much creativity precedes the franchisee, there is still creative work to be done—like generating success, for example.

Franchisors know from experience most good ideas come from their innovative franchisees. In my experience, both as a director of an international franchisor and as a franchisee, at least 90 percent of the important marketing, financial, and operational innovations come from the franchisee. Although the franchisor created the concept, the entrepreneurial partner is still the primary idea source, the innovator. Highly innovative operators are a godsend for franchisors. Their contribution to the system's success is significant.

Franchisees aren't robots. The opportunities to create success are as plentiful within a franchised business as in a non-franchised business. In some cases the opportunities to have impact are even greater, as innovations can be adopted throughout the system. A franchising concept, like other businesses, ultimately thrives in proportion to the talent it's able to attract.

III

ACHIEVING THROUGH SELECTING, TRAINING AND MEASURING HUMAN RESOURCES

"In the global economic boom of the 1990s, human resources are the competitive edge for both companies and countries. In the global economic competition of the information economy, the quality and innovativeness of human resources will spell the difference."

— *Megatrends 2000*

John Naisbitt and Patricia Aburdene weren't kidding when they included the above statement in *Megatrends 2000*. The first of the 10 megatrends they forecast for this decade is a global economic boom—and their discussion clearly identifies a link between organizational success and *avant garde* human resource thinking.

This chapter focuses on a specialized area of human resource development. It makes suggestions that are off the beaten path of most small- and medium-sized businesses. It suggests new, more professional, and futuristic ways to do old things. And it offers opportunities for leaders and achieving organizations that will improve their ability to select and effectively supervise their most important asset—talented people.

HUMAN RESOURCE HABIT 1

The Hiring Habit

The most effective way to impact employee character, and therefore the ethics of your business, is on the way in.

W. Michael Blumenthal, former Treasury Secretary, told *Business Week* he made the biggest hiring mistakes of his 36 year career when he "put intelligence and energy ahead of morality." He continued, "In choosing people, you have to try to make sure they have a clear sense of what is right and wrong, a willingness to be truthful, the courage to say what they think and to do what they think is right, even if the politics mitigate against that. This is the quality that really should be at the top.

"I'm saying that I was too often impressed by the high intelligence and the substantive knowledge of an individual and did not always pay enough attention to the question of how honest, how courageous and how good a person the individual really was," Blumenthal concluded.

If you use the selection ideas and tools discussed in this chapter to give yourself an organization full of people strong in the characteristics Blumenthal discusses, you'll do fine. Character counts.

HUMAN RESOURCE HABIT 2

Getting the Selection Edge

"All successful employers are stalking people who will do the unusual, people who think, people who attract attention by performing more than is expected of them."

— *Charles Schwab*

Selecting the right people is the life line of achievement. We can do everything else right, but if we miss this one, we might as well hang up the cleats. We can't play the game of high achievement effectively unless we know how to select talent.

Our legalistic society, the high cost of recruiting and training, and the shrinking labor pool make guesswork expensive. When we hire, review, promote or terminate, we need to know what we're doing—and have some basis upon which to support our decision.

I spent much of the last decade looking for the selection edge. I knew hiring and selection decisions were a combination of thorough inquiry and judgment and I was responsible for both. But I also knew there was fierce competition for the good people. We weren't the only growing business looking for them! Was there a system, a method that could help?

A recent meeting with Ken Muir, President of PES Profile Evaluation Systems in Vancouver, British Columbia, gave me hope. Muir's company is the marketer of the *Profile Evaluation System*, distributed in the U.S. by Leadership Management, Inc.

of Waco, Texas. More than 300,000 people worldwide have been profiled by PES, which can provide tailored insight into any of 27 job descriptions. PES is currently undergoing a comprehensive one million dollar revalidation, making it the most validated evaluation tool on the market.

Many organizations find the greatest human resource challenge of all is in marketing and sales. Accurately selecting people who will become sales achievers is a task somewhere between challenging and impossible. Too often it's guesswork. And even when we guess right we frequently mess it up at promotion time, wrongly assuming the best salesperson will make the best sales manager.

Fortunately, sales achievement forecasting is also benefiting from the growth in personnel profiling. Certainly one of the best sales profiling tools on the market is the Sales Success Profile. Inexpensive and easy to administer, it provides feedback on 12 sales aptitude areas and gives a clear *rating* of sales ability. Developed by Lousig-Nont & Associates, it is a valuable instrument for measuring both inside/retail and outside sales aptitudes. I have found it to be highly predictive.

Beyond initial selection assistance lies a potentially more important evaluation benefit. Supervisors frequently find it difficult to communicate with staff. Especially when it's time for review, promotion, or when emerging problems make coaching and counseling a highly productive activity. Having an employee's personality and mental profile available removes some of the intimidation supervisors feel. Profiling and evaluation provide considerable insight into the employee. It creates a broad agenda of topics to discuss when coaching, reviewing, or seeking the proper candidate for promotion. A formal evaluation process can be a significant contributor to effective supervision.

Another benefit is the capability to personalize and customize. For example, let's assume you have a 10-person sales staff. Among them are five achievers, three who are mediocre, and two who are marginal. One way to grow your organization is to find a way to *clone* the five achievers. This is easily done with some evaluation services. Profiling and building a normative pattern of the five achievers provides the mold.

Using normative behavioral patterns as a guide, you can match the profiles of employment candidates with your achievers and integrate the results into the other elements of your hiring decision. Developing this information base will yield a higher probability of hiring success.

Most evaluation tools measure personality characteristics, some measure mental aptitudes, and a few, like PES, include the validity-checking step that provides assurance the evaluation has integrity. All three areas are important, although hourly or low skill employees can be evaluated on personality characteristics only.

The computer is playing a major role in the rapidly increasing use of formal employee evaluation. For example, most services sell user-friendly software which allows easy accomplishment of both administration and in-house scoring. Many employers have wanted to incorporate profiling into their human resource activities but have stayed away because of cost, confusion, or intimidation. Now it's simple and affordable for most businesses.

Profiling your finalist employment candidates, as well as those already on staff, is an important area of opportunity for achieving organizations. It reduces guesswork, helps you know your people better, improves the quality of communication, reduces fear of lawsuits for discrimination or inappropriate dismissal, and helps you find more people like your top producers. All of these opportunities, until recently, were available only to larger organizations.

HUMAN RESOURCE HABIT 3

"ATR" Is One of the ABC's of Success

"We are what we repeatedly do. Excellence, then, is not an act but a habit."

In this decade, and into the next century, personal and organizational achievement require us to develop methods to identify and attract good people earlier than our competition. We must train them perpetually and design our business in a way that makes them want to stay.

When asked what I do for a living, my shorthand answer is, "I'm in the ATR business." A is for *attracting* talent, T is for *training* talent, and R is for *retaining* talent. If there are simple definitions of achieving, ATR heads the list.

For years American business has hailed people as our most important asset. Too bad we really didn't believe it until recently. Our new-found understanding isn't a result of profound enlightenment. We became believers only when faced with startling details on demographic changes and inadequacies in our schools. We got some religion when the abundance of qualified applicants disappeared.

Reality is indeed startling. In 1991, American business spent an estimated $210 billion dollars on formal and informal training, yet less than 15 percent of our work force received any formal job-related training. There's lots of room for improvement, and this is the decade we'll begin to see it. Today's level of training is insignificant compared to what we'll be providing in 10 years.

If you are in a leadership position and intend to lead an organization that has the capacity to succeed, you will increase your training budget, not only in absolute dollars but as a percentage of revenues. Some of the enlightened will do it because they understand the opportunity, although most will do it under duress and out of last-ditch necessity. Increased training needs represent a basic cultural adjustment from the long-standing assumption that training is the responsibility of our schools.

Effective organizations will more and more mirror the diversity of the people using their product or service. If a demographically older audience uses a product, the work force making it might also be older. If Hispanics consume the service, the company providing the service will be representatively Hispanic. If the product focuses on a young demographic, the people designing the product will have similar characteristics.

This *mirroring* effect and the diversity of employees it suggests, will further increase the need for—and reliance on—training for years to come. The increasing diversity of the work force will also require more flexible, more entrepreneurial management practices.

The leading organizations of tomorrow will be those willing to change, to look at their opportunities flexibly and entrepreneurially. They will put *people* at the top of their list of important assets.

Training Trends

It's easy to document that training and skill development is a dynamic need area. How we choose to go about providing it is a subject of varied opinion. Many new training techniques and philosophies will emerge as we feel our way along. Among them will be:

1) More precise training needs analysis.

2) Growing belief in the need for, and desirability of, training repetition.

John Shand, a forward-looking human resource consultant who leads Performance Development, Inc. in Charlotte, North Carolina, refers to the "surgery syndrome" in discussing the inefficiencies of untargeted training. Shand says too much training is done without adequately identifying specific areas of need. This approach is much like a brain surgeon shaking hands with a patient and saying, "Hi, I'm a brain surgeon and you need brain surgery." In the training business, as in medicine, there's a need to take an x-ray first. The training x-ray is administered through formal profiling and evaluation.

When suggesting that training be based on formally identified, targeted needs, it is appropriate to suggest the human resource consultant understand his own limitations. A formal training needs analysis will sometimes propose training he's not capable of effectively providing. When that happens, the consultant/trainer should act in the client's best interest, even when it means referring business to another trainer. In other words, the human resource consultant should be willing to unbundle the training needs analysis and the training itself.

The second training trend identified above is a growing belief in the need for, and desirability of, training repetition. This tendency is one I thoroughly believe in. My introduction to Paul J. Meyer, founder of Success Motivation Institute (SMI) and Leadership Management, Inc. (LMI), created this belief. Meyer has had a profound impact on my training philosophies. Mr. Meyer is one of America's profound thinkers. For years he has consistently preached his theory of spaced training repetition and applied it to the many training programs he has authored and marketed worldwide. Spaced repetition merely proposes we will not retain more than 10 percent of what we see or hear the first time we see or hear it in a training environment. While we would like to believe otherwise, that's the way it is.

Shortly after meeting Paul Meyer, I had an opportunity to test his spaced repetition theory. While visiting our restaurant operation in Des Moines, I met with our training director. Chris Riddle has been with us many years as a capable restaurant manager, but was new to the training slot. To say he was frustrated is an understatement. He is an achiever who was pulling his hair out.

Chris' job description included conducting an introductory training course required of new employees before they work in a restaurant. At the course conclusion everyone took a test. Their scores were uniformly good. Yet when the new employees went into a restaurant they had trouble doing what the test said they were prepared to do.

Our general manager, operations manager, and Chris joined me the next morning for a two hour session on spaced repetition. We reformulated our entire training philosophy that morning based on the realities of learning retention and the need for spaced repetition. We continued the introductory training as before but scheduled everyone back, at spaced intervals, three more times over a four-week period to review all materials.

It has made a significant difference in the way we teach, our training expectations, and the knowledge our people have. Spaced repetition changed our organization and transformed a self-doubting training director concerned about his effectiveness into a confident, effective teacher.

Consider your own seminar experiences. If you are like me you have attended many. You thought the material presented was, more often than not, pretty good stuff. How much of it did you remember? What percentage did you put to use?

Now imagine attending that seminar every week for five weeks. How much higher would your retention be? How much more valuable would the information be to you? Most of us will not remember more than 10 percent of the information during each exposure. To retain 50 percent of a seminar's potential, therefore, we would need to attend the seminar five times. If seminars were set up to train us repetitively—and we were willing to attend repetitively—our learning curve would increase dramatically.

As new training programs and concepts are developed, look for increasing emphasis on the Paul J. Meyer spaced repetition philosophy. It really works.

HUMAN RESOURCE HABIT 4

Good Interviews Are Easy, Bad Ones Are Tough

I love to conduct job interviews. One of my really good feelings is having the opportunity to listen to talented people talk about themselves. However, interviewers confuse me. They act as though they want to hire more than the applicant wants the job.

Most of us don't interview regularly. When we do, it's often done in a frenzied environment that isn't conducive to sound decision-making. These *Twelve Techniques Toward Interview Truth* can make interviewing job applicants more fun and effective.

1. *Listen, don't talk.* You need to learn, not teach. Interviewers are often too *salesy* and talk too much. Remain still, attentive, and challenge yourself to keep your mouth shut. Relax, sit back, and let the interviewee do the talking.

2. *Buy, don't sell.* I'm astonished by how many interviewers put on their selling shoes before the interview is over. The prospect will want the position more if you give signals that many individuals seek the opening. Well into the interview process, when you know who you want, you can open up a little and sell your organization. Until then, be a buyer. Force the interviewee to sell.

3. *Don't share all your sins.* Hey, your organization isn't perfect, but there's no need to talk about corporate acne. They'll find out soon enough. Effective interviewers present themselves and their organizations in as good a light as they legitimately can.

4. *Have tolerance for the unusual person.* It's sometimes the unconventional applicant who has the most potential. Don't reach your conclusions too early or too emotionally.

5. *Facts and truth aren't synonyms.* Facts, such as numbers, can intentionally mislead. Close listening and precise follow up questions will help find the truth—but you may have to reach for it. Remember, an applicant who knows what he or she is doing is selling.

6. *Behavior repeats itself.* We've all interviewed the person who was fired as many times as hired. It's always someone else's fault, of course. Behavior is predictable and repetitive. Watch out.

7. *Ask the question, "What have you accomplished that has been unusual?"* Most of the time, you'll get a blank stare or a paragraph of baloney. Occasionally, however, this question will cause an interviewee's eyes to light up like the Las Vegas strip. When this happens, make sure you've got his or her telephone number.

8. *Invite talent.* Too many interviewers are leery of hiring people they fear might be smarter or more talented than they are. There's a direct correlation between talent and achievement. How can the interviewer not be interested?

9. *To find out, ask.* Go for the jugular if necessary to get direct, unhedged answers. If responses are indirect, persist with follow up questions. Take control of the interview and the answers will come.

10. *Always ask indirect questions.* The burden of talking should be on the applicant. Phrase your indirect question in a way that the applicant can't answer by "yes" or "no." Require

them to expound in more detail. Phrases such as "tell me about" work well.

11. *Be more interested in the person than the position.* Steven Jobs of Apple Computer fame said he tried to find exceptional talent, then looked for something for them to do. His point is valid. Too many times we turn away capable people in favor of a mediocre hire because he or she fits the *exact* slot better. Talent is the name of the game. If you get enough of it and know how to cultivate it, you are going to do well.

    Some people have it. Some don't. The business of hiring and keeping talent is the profession every achieving business person should be in.

12. *Check basic skills.* Spelling and writing are important skills, but it's amazing how many applicants do neither well. It's also shocking how few prospective employers bother to check!

    We give all applicants a spelling test as part of the initial interview. I hope the test, reproduced on page 91, is of as much value to your skill analysis as it has been to ours.

HUMAN RESOURCE HABIT 5

Candidate Selection Spelling Test

Instruction: Some of the words on the following page are correctly spelled and some are not (answers provided on page 92).

The employment provisions of the Americans with Disabilities Act (ADA) require employers with 15 of more employees to be prepared to provide "reasonable accommodation" (such as oral administration to a candidate with a reading disability) when using assessment tools. In fact, some states have adopted disability provisions applying to *all* employers, regardless of size. So it's important to be familiar not only with the federal law but with the disability provisions of your state as well.

Candidates who miss four or less are good spellers. When more than eight are missed, spelling is marginal and, depending on job description, could present job performance problems.

already _____   convenient _____

goverment _____   referance _____

accidant _____   fourty _____

deside _____   nuisence _____

accept _____   beleive _____

committe _____   guaranteed _____

bussiness _____   definitly _____

minute _____   ninth _____

realy _____   permenent _____

invoise _____   apologize _____

consideration _____   remittance _____

assure _____   immediatly _____

foriegn _____   morgage _____

responsability _____   bookeeping _____

application _____   desireable _____

develope _____   withhold _____

issue _____   recomend _____

receive _____   acknowlege _____

agreement _____   aquainted _____

arrangment _____   proceed _____

experiance _____   ledger _____

charactor _____   hastely _____

already _____		convenient _____	
goverment _____	government	referance _____	reference
accidant _____	accident	fourty _____	forty
deside _____	decide	nuisence _____	nuisance
accept _____		beleive _____	believe
committe _____	committee	guaranteed _____	
bussiness _____	business	definitly _____	definitely
minute _____		ninth _____	
realy _____	really	permenent _____	permanent
invoise _____	invoice	apologize _____	
consideration _____		remittance _____	
assure _____		immediatly _____	immediately
foriegn _____	foreign	morgage _____	mortgage
responsability _____	responsibility	bookeeping _____	bookkeeping
application _____		desireable _____	desirable
develope _____	develop	withhold _____	
issue _____		recomend _____	recommend
receive _____		acknowlege _____	acknowledge
agreement _____		aquainted _____	acquainted
arrangment _____	arrangement	proceed _____	
experiance _____	experience	ledger _____	
charactor _____	character	hastely _____	hastily

HUMAN RESOURCE HABIT 6

Twenty Penetrating Questions Worth Asking in a Serious Interview

The quality of your job interview can be no better than the quality of your questions. Although my interviews are thorough and challenging, I've had interviewees tell me it was the most rewarding interview time they ever spent.

The purpose of a question is to provide the interviewer with as much information as possible. Here are 20 questions that will accomplish those goals.

1. Based on what you now know, describe your level of interest in our position (initial commitment check).

2. Discuss your familiarity with our organization.

3. If you were in my place, what would you look for in the person filling this position?

4. Describe how you spent a typical day in your previous (current) position.

5. What were your most significant accomplishments in your last (current) position?

6. What three responsibilities did you enjoy most in your last (current) position?

7. Tell me specifically why you left (want to leave) your last (current) position.

8. Describe your last/present supervisor.

9. Describe the nicest compliment you've received and why you received it.

10. What have you been criticized for?

11. If I picked up the phone right now and called your last supervisor (use name if available) what would he/she say about you?

12. Describe the perfect boss.

13. Are you ready to be responsible for your own results?

14. What personal and professional achievements are you most proud of?

15. What are your most important personal goals (away from the office)?

16. What are your most important professional goals?

17. To what extent have you participated in the creation or execution of a strategic plan?

18. What are you willing to do to be successful in the future, that you haven't been willing to do in the past?

19. Why should we choose you?

20. Based on your current level of knowledge about this position, describe your level of interest (concluding commitment check). The strength of their response to this question is critical.

Please note these questions are all indirect, thus discouraging a yes or no answer. And every one is designed to get the interviewee to do the talking.

HUMAN RESOURCE HABIT 7

The Art of Measuring Talent

"We have a preference for people who are likely to leave their imprint on our time."

— *Arthur Koestler*
The Anatomy of Snobbery

Perfecting the art of measuring employee imprint is a singularly important business opportunity. Effective, skillful job measurement can transform an organization from mediocrity to excellence. Measurement improves performance. That's why achieving organizations are careful to measure their talent frequently and effectively.

We need to have expectations of people. What's more important is understanding them well enough to have the *right* expectations. Developing understanding requires communication.

Everyone does something well. We need to find what their something is. When we don't know, we risk putting the right people in the wrong slot. This not only reduces the employee's opportunity for growth but the organization's profit.

Effective measurement begins with knowledge. In the future, much of it will be provided by formal profiling and evaluation. Knowing people improves understanding what they want, what brings them satisfaction, and at what speed they learn. It also positions the observer to look for glimpses of excellence, situations where they're operating comfortably within their own system of success.

We perceive the ideal working environment as a group of people at peace and without conflict. In at least one respect, that's not ideal. Talent becomes discontented when results fall short of expectations. If the leader is fair-minded and the employee is reasonable (nobody likes arrogance or prima donnas), measurement can turn discontent into something positive for both parties. For the business, it's an opportunity to learn about expectations; for the employee, an opportunity to communicate the problem. It's a cooperative effort leading to mutual understanding.

Too many supervisors shortchange employees, passing them off as naturally lazy, as folks wanting to get off as easily as possible. While that's true in some cases, most have enough motivation and energy to meet any reasonable expectation. That's the key. The supervisor is responsible for setting expectations. What we expect is what we get. Success doesn't happen until somebody expects it.

Real achievement can't exist without expectation. A critical aspect of leadership is to see that expectations are in place.

A talented person can be defined as someone having the capacity for excellent performance. However, talent is maximized only in tandem with an expectation. Expectation must be within the ability of the available talent, or we simply have a square peg in a round hole. Don Clifton, founder of Selection Research, Inc. in Lincoln, Nebraska, refers to the importance of having the right expectations. He suggests that we "shouldn't try to make a pig sing—all we'll accomplish is making ourselves mad and frustrate the hell out of the pig."

Predictability is another requirement of effective measurement. Talented people not only want to know how they're doing but need security that expectations have purposeful continuity and predictability. This requires the presence of a predictable leader whose goals transcend periodic emotionalism or lapses in judgment.

Predictable leaders aren't predictable by accident. In addition to having deeply-held philosophies, they enhance their predictability by working from a strategic plan that serves as an organizational guidepost.

Our identification of talent begins during the hiring interview. One trait of the talented interviewee is spontaneous recall. The applicant who is asked challenging interview questions, and who responds adroitly, is providing a first clue that extraordinary talent may be present.

Talent identification is also performance related. High achievement isn't an aberration. It's a predictable, recurring, consistent, and observable behavioral pattern. Appearance, punctuality, behavior toward superiors or underlings, reliability, predictability, etc. are unchanging. They are indelible patterns of life. Watch for them.

Accept the probability that such living patterns are permanent. This will minimize our attempts to "make the pig sing." As former Oklahoma football coach, Barry Switzer, said, "When the whistle blows, the great players play." And, I would add, the poor players don't.

Rules of Effective Measurement

There are only three, but they are the foundation upon which good measurement technique depends:

1. *Keep it understandable and objective.* If the employee can't readily understand it, change it. Objectivity requires an arithmetic calculation, not an opinion or subjective estimation.

2. *Differentiate between busy-ness and productivity.* It's easy for someone to look busy. That game is an art form for some. What and how much gets done is the important factor.

3. *Measure the work, not the worker.* Emotions creep into every human relationship, but effective measurement requires that we be as unemotional as possible. The question is not how much you like the person—it's how much you like the person's work. When measuring performance,

measure the work. It's counterproductive to measure the worker.

HUMAN RESOURCE
HABIT 8

Creating an Effective Measurement Philosophy

Most businesses have job descriptions, a document communicating what a person is to accomplish. You might say it describes what someone is paid to do.

Imagine an unusual, but well-organized business, unique because it doesn't have job descriptions. How would its leaders communicate to employees what they were paid to do? Is it possible? You bet it is! It's done through an incentive compensation plan. The paycheck becomes the report card.

A good job description and a good compensation plan should accomplish the same goal. Are both needed? Rather than spend time designing sheets of paper with requirements on them, why not sit down with the employee and discuss what you want done and create an incentive plan that motivates the person to do it?

Determine what you want accomplished, then find an effective, motivating way to reward for it. You'll discover the traditional job description is no longer necessary. What's better than giving the employee an automatic performance review with every paycheck? You will find people automatically doing what they get paid to do.

Everyone wants positive motivational leverage on their money. That's exactly what happens when compensation is aligned with responsibility. An effectively aligned incentive compensation package can:

Increase profitability

Increase responsiveness to customers

Increase individual and team productivity

Provide important performance feedback to employees

Provide employees with a record of performance

Increase PEP—Per Employee Productivity

Increase variable, reduce fixed payroll cost

Provide constant reinforcement of successes

Increase employee motivation

HUMAN RESOURCE HABIT 9

Creating an Effective Measurement System

Measurement is not arbitrary, subjective, or random. It is formal, specific, arithmetic, and predictable. It starts with the accounting department.

The most important principle in effective measurement is that the organization be able to produce the data reflecting the measurements. Measurement requires a collaboration of accounting and supervising personnel who collectively determine:

1) What supervisors want measured.

2) What accounting says can be measured.

The list of measurement opportunities is endless. Here are just a few to whet your appetite:

INDIVIDUAL BEST

new accounts
total tickets written
total volume
budget achievement
percentage of goal
sales of specific product
sales contracts
best volume period

TEAM BEST

ten best profit months
ten best sales months
highest sales for each calendar month
highest profit for each calendar month
highest profit margins for each calendar month
best day volume

These examples are only a starting point. Be creative. Ask your people for ideas. Consider all opportunities and choose among them. Many of the individual measurements also work for the team and vice versa.

Celebrate! Achievement dies in a vacuum, celebration gives it life. Don't merely record—reward. You don't have to buy a plaque each time there is a significant achievement. But acknowledge it and communicate it to the organization with excitement and pleasure.

HUMAN RESOURCE HABIT 10

The Firing Fallacy

We think of firing someone as a totally negative experience. It's not.

Termination is just as often a confirmation of strength as it is a sign of weakness. Firing can be good for both parties provided the proper humanitarian and legal guidelines are followed.

What's worse than an organization wasting money employing someone who doesn't fit? Or an employee "serving time" in an organization that doesn't suit his or her aptitude or style?

While not proposing that firing someone is an act of humanity, it is often more humanitarian than keeping the person around. Doing so prevents the individual from achieving something of value in an alternative environment.

There are times when an involuntary termination is in the best interests of both parties. The time has passed when enlightened companies hold on to people to be good guys. To keep an able-bodied but ineffective person is a disservice to the potential of both parties. The way to control turnover and protect the interests of both the organization and the individual is to have a tough, thorough selection process. Making it tough to get in reduces traffic on the way out.

IV

ACHIEVING THROUGH PEOPLE

"If you want one year of prosperity, grow rain. If you want ten years of prosperity, grow trees. If you want one hundred years of prosperity, grow people."
— *Chinese Proverb*

Some say the work ethic is dead. In a survey by the Institute of Industrial Engineers, three out of four engineers said workers in our country have lost their strong work ethic. Obviously this contributes to low productivity. The survey concluded workers aren't working hard or effectively and lack the loyalty and motivation workers had as recently as 1980.

The survey responses criticized management for lacking the commitment to find ways to encourage employee productivity. They concluded that linking pay to performance and profit would increase productivity. Amen!

PEOPLE HABIT 1

Two P's in a Pod— Performance and Productivity

"Find out what people do well, and let them do a lot of it."

Business is a sinner. We create and allow working environments where people aren't productive to their potential. An employee who puts out 100 percent is happier than one getting by at 70 percent. Putting one's heart and soul into an assignment is less tiring than coasting. Busy people are more creative, energetic, enthusiastic, and productive. Imagine being underemployed. What kind of feelings would you have about your abilities, your chances for promotion, or financial progress? Odds are they wouldn't be positive.

People participate in distracting activities when they aren't busy. They become involved in office politics, grow defensive, and form personal power bases to increase their feeling of job security.

Too often we restrict performance and productivity by having too many people doing too little. Ask fewer people to do more. Allow them to perform to their potential. They will feel good about it. Most of America's work force would rather their supervisors depend upon them too much than too little. Productive work environments exist where every participant is fully engaged. Each feels important because he or she is making a needed contribution.

What are you doing to maximize performance and productivity? What productivity level do you require? What incentives do you provide? Are you part of the problem or part of the solution?

Let's not look to the other guy. We can talk all day about the quality of workers. Let's look at the quality of leadership. Many employers are under-utilizing workers within a system that has inadequate expectations and fails to link productivity to pay.

Surprisingly, when given a choice between challenge and boredom, many people will choose challenge. Don't let them down.

PEOPLE HABIT 2

If You Have Thoroughbreds in Your Stable Let 'Em Run

> *"The difference between a successful person and others is not a lack of strength, not a lack of knowledge, but rather a lack of will."*

What we achieve in life is to a large extent proportional to what we allow others to achieve.

Thoroughbreds have a mental edge, a constant urge to reach for higher levels of achievement and an ability to get pumped for the big game. Diluting these championship characteristics because a parent, coach, or leader does not play a supportive role is tragic.

I had a college buddy who was a fireball salesman. After graduating, my friend joined a major computer firm. He was assigned a large, underachieving territory and given a goal of doubling sales within three years. He swallowed hard to digest his budget, rolled up his sleeves, put on his go-getter attitude, and went to work.

In less than three years he not only doubled territory sales—he increased them more than *tenfold*. It was a super achievement. He had an incentive package, and his production created substantial incentive income. As it turned out, too substantial! He committed the cardinal sin of making more than his boss.

He was an exceptional salesman, and unlike many sales-types, knew himself well enough to know he was happiest when selling. Like many companies, his employer wrongly believed that good salespeople make good managers. So they offered him a management position—at decreased pay. He turned it down, asking them only to allow him to continue developing his territory.

That wasn't acceptable to his employer. They cut his territory in half, which slashed his income by 30 percent. They dangled the carrot for him to get his income back up to its previous level (of course, then they would cut his territory again).

Three months later he resigned and joined a start-up competitor. He has been causing his former employer fits ever since.

Many large, non-entrepreneurial organizations have unwritten rules. One of them is—don't be too good, or you'll get penalized. Another is that you can't make more than your boss.

The "we've got to hold the thoroughbred down" mentality isn't the sole property of larger companies. I've seen dozens of situations in smaller, supposedly entrepreneurial organizations where the owner-entrepreneur stifles achievement by rearranging territories, responsibilities and pay schedules to massage free market results. These efforts level the achievement curve, pull the overachiever down, and make the average worker look better.

Entrepreneurial leaders do not seek to level the achievement curve. They fight policies that do. An organization can accomplish lofty goals only if able to attract achieving people who make it happen.

If you attract talent, you can do anything. If you don't, you will accomplish much less. When you find thoroughbreds, let them run! They will win—not only for themselves but for you.

PEOPLE HABIT 3

The Art of Empowerment

Empower: enable, invest, deputize, endow, authorize, arm

"The hardest instrument to play is second fiddle."

We have difficulty empowering others. Our professional world centers on ourselves and our own abilities. Entrepreneurial delegation is infrequent, empowerment unusual.

Achieving entrepreneurial leaders, however, have learned the advantages of including others in their exciting world. Not only are associates involved, they participate in achievement they can call their own. Achieving leaders work to make others around them feel strong, responsible, and needed. They keep the scoreboard in sight, the team names always posted. Success isn't lonely in this environment. It's exciting when everyone wins.

When people are given liberty to use their ability, the talent put to use on behalf of the enterprise increases geometrically. Positive feelings become contagious, people help each other succeed, and achievement rises to heights not found in most organizations.

Empowerment requires giving, a trait typical of good leaders. It's not, however, a trait typical to managers who seek to sustain and increase their importance by diminishing that of others.

Like most entrepreneurs, I'm a corporate dropout. Early in my professional life I experienced life in the unempowered lane. It wasn't fun.

Having sorted out my thoughts over the years, I now understand that my corporate experience consisted of responsibility without authority. The "branch manager" title I held wasn't much more than that, a title. Our office was really run by a CEO-seeker at headquarters more intent on building his personal reputation than empowering those reporting to him. I watched him dig tunnels under the working environment of my peers. It was a painful yet enlightening and educational experience. I learned all about being *un*empowered. When I became an entrepreneur, I vowed to remember what it felt like to have large responsibility with little authority.

Empower others by inviting all employees to join the team. Help them keep score. Involve them in the free enterprise system and the feelings of responsibility and importance that go with it. Allow learning through failure. When accomplishments are made be willing to say, "You did it."

Everyone who does a hard day's work deserves to smell the aroma of success. It's a smell they'll want more often.

PEOPLE HABIT 4

Decentralize the Decision

There are managers who feel a need to know every detail. They experience discomfort when assigning a task to someone else. On the other hand, there are employees who doubt the abilities of anyone who doesn't know every detail of the organization's life.

Two years ago I was visiting with an employee about our company's plans. He asked me a question I didn't have the answer to, so I suggested he contact his immediate supervisor. I could tell from the employee's look that he was put off when I wasn't able to respond on the spot.

Trying to relieve his tension, I bluntly asked if he thought I should know the answer to his question. His response? "You're the president of the company. You should know everything." Yes, I'm the president of the company, but I don't know every detail about every aspect of our business. And I don't want to.

What kind of organization would we have if I was familiar with every detail? We would have an environment where one person ran everything. If every decision, regardless of importance, required my approval, we would suffer organizational gridlock.

We would also have a hierarchical structure without empowered people. They couldn't grow and would not be allowed to make choices. In a nutshell, it would be a disaster.

Leaders who have created effective organizations understand it is neither necessary nor possible to have complete knowledge of what everyone does or what they are accountable for. Instead, the leader delegates responsibilities, hoping to create a bond of mutual trust between employee and employer.

The prevailing wisdom in our business culture is that the leader should be present to maximize organizational potential. I believe the opposite is true—*a leader doesn't know how good he is until he's gone.* If he leads a decentralized organization with people who think for themselves and make decisions as necessary, the organization will function well in the leader's absence.

The decentralization of the organization and the resulting empowerment of people is, perhaps more than anything else, the factor that differentiates the *effective leader* from a mundane manager.

PEOPLE HABIT 5

Uncovering a Well-Kept Secret

The American business community is suffering from a serious, self-inflicted wound. We're applying the tourniquet, but it's painfully late.

Even our top corporate leaders succumbed to the ease of adding jobs to accommodate growth. It became a habit richly ingrained in our business culture. To add employees was a badge of growth and progress. At meetings and conventions corporate department heads bubbled with pride when telling audiences how many people the department added since the last meeting. More people meant growth. And growth meant progress. But only for a while.

We're now paying the price. Day after day, headline after headline, we read of company after company laying off workers. "Downsizing" is a new buzz-word in our business vocabulary.

The excesses of yesterday are taking their toll on companies and people, many of whom thought productivity was optional. Business is learning if you throw too many people at growth, someday you'll be throwing them out the door.

Bill Byrne

PEOPLE HABIT 6

The Inequity of Equity
Part I
The Employee Perspective

While Harvey Mackay was going for a *Swim With The Sharks*, he wrote a lesson entitled "Owning 1 Percent Of Something Is Worth More Than Managing 100 Percent Of Anything." Excuse me, Harvey. I disagree.

The basis for my disagreement isn't founded in selfishness or disregard for the employee. On the contrary, it's because I highly regard the value of the employee.

Following my speech to a business group, a middle-aged businessman approached to shake my hand and ask a few questions. We had a brief chat, and after several interruptions we walked to the coffee shop to continue our conversation. As we chatted over coffee, a panoramic view of his business life unfolded.

Jim was an energetic, enthusiastic, and ostensibly capable person. He was especially proud of one accomplishment—he was not just the manager of his clothing store, he was the "managing partner."

I inquired about his ownership, "How much do you own?"

Jim proudly said 10 percent.

"How much is your 10 percent worth?"

He didn't know, "but the major owner says he keeps track of it."

"What happens if you find a better job that you want to take advantage of?"

Jim reflected on that, finally telling me he thought his partner would offer him a fair amount if that ever happened.

I then asked, "Jim, what's a fair amount?"

Again, Jim relied on his partner to determine the amount.

Our conversation totalled about 45 minutes, and when it was over I came clean. I told him what his 10 percent was worth. I told him it was worth very little, perhaps nothing.

There are thousands of *managing partners* in Jim's situation. Few understand what they have, or more likely, what they don't have.

Stock ownership has its privileges—a stock certificate, a periodic valuation of a share's worth, a business continuity agreement. Unless structured otherwise, there's also a voting right—in theory an opportunity to have some control over the company.

But chances are better than even the "major partner" was using Jim, either with intent or by negligence. Ownership not only has privileges, it has prerequisites. Among those are documentation and formalization. If not in written binding form, *partnership* and *ownership* are hollow words. Even when cast in writing, a minority interest in a privately-held firm is less valuable than most minor partners believe.

Another alternative—business continuity agreements (discussed fully in Chapter IX)—state a value which is ideally funded by life insurance. Why life insurance? Because it provides funding at death. In the real world, the minority partner who's without documentation and formalization will receive precious little when he or she leaves the business.

Although you are in a stronger position when appropriate agreements are in place, the full valuation of any minority ownership is always at risk. Majority owners will often negotiate the value with a departing minority partner. Usually the minority value is less than what the agreement states. That's because the marketplace accords a higher value to majority stock and because business continuity agreements concern themselves primarily with disposition at death.

Too much of the time, minority ownership is symbolic. The reality is most *managing partners* don't have a legal leg to stand on. When they do, it's frequently only at death.

Partner-employees can avoid the trap of "symbolic ownership" by requiring that formal business continuity agreements be in place. And that the agreement provide exit valuations—not only at death, but when living.

While the minority partner-employee takes the brunt of the symbolic ownership punch, minority partnerships are seldom beneficial to the majority owner or the business.

Ownership is a strong, compelling word. It has magic. Magic, however, is an illusion. The minority owner, the partner-employee, the managing partner—use the title you wish—should keep this in mind. Minority ownership isn't what it appears. There are better ways. Keep reading.

PEOPLE HABIT 7

The Inequity of Equity
Part II
The Employer Perspective

As discussed in Part I, minority equity isn't always beneficial to the employee of the privately-held company. In most cases it's not good for the majority owner, either.

The reason is simple—it creates too many problems. Providing a piece of the action is easy. Living up to the ethical, financial, and legal obligations that go with it is not. Nor is it always done.

Why is employee equity offered? It usually relates to motivation and retention. Businesses need key employees to create growth, profit, and wealth. Success requires finding and keeping talent. No wonder the ownership carrot dangles so frequently.

Passing out small pieces of ownership is a cheap, expedient answer to the perpetual question, "How can I keep them here and keep them happy?" Yet other opportunities exist, most of which are not only more creative but more enlightened.

The wants of the workplace are the same as always. Employees want good pay, complete benefits, job security, a stimulating environment, to work with likeable people, etc. It's not only what the marketplace requires, it's what employees deserve.

Some employees, however, want more. They want to emulate the employer. They want to think, participate and feel important. They want to take pride in what they do and pleasure in their success. They go out of their way for the boss. It's only fair the boss return the favor. Too often, that *favor* is stock incentive in the form of minority stock ownership. Some owners hand out privately-held stock like it was worthless. Unfortunately, sometimes it is.

When a stockholder awards stock, it's more than sharing a piece of paper. It's a pledge. When that pledge is broken, for whatever reason, it's a mistake with serious consequences.

One pitfall of the minority stock ownership incentive in privately-held organizations is the business is seldom set up to do it right. Inadequate documentation, poor design, and willy-nilly corporate execution of legal requirements top the list.

The stock incentive is one of two primary incentive concepts. The other is cash-based, and there are literally hundreds of adaptations of each.

Stock incentives can be troublemakers for the privately-held company. Most stock incentives are improperly designed and administered. They create more problems than they solve. Issuing privately-held minority stock to an employee has, for many, been operationally and legally disruptive.

In reality, many business owners are willing to give stock because they don't think it will ever be worth anything significant. Lawyers love to find stock incentives in privately-held firms. That's one good reason the rest of us shouldn't.

An employee sees the stock incentive formula as complicated, ambiguous, and probably showing favor to other employees. Cash incentives significantly reduce these problems. From the employee perspective, cash is tangible. Those who sincerely want to achieve excellence in a privately-held organization should think cash when thinking incentives.

Effective incentive plans have several of the following common denominators:

1. The plan is formal and written. It is fully understood by those who participate.

2. It is objectively measurable and readily definable in dollars.

3. It is substantial enough to be important to participating employees.

4. It is fair, providing appropriate levels of participation for all employees.

5. It considers both earnings and tenure.

6. A person or persons who employees trust makes calculations.

7. The distributions are frequent, monthly if possible.

8. Regular communication about the plan is scheduled.

———————

PEOPLE HABIT 8

The Inequity of Equity
Part III
The Tax Deferred Perspective

In addition to arranging plans that provide employees with the right to participate in current profits, consider providing deferred profit participation. This is usually a very selective benefit reserved only for key employees.

The plan should provide a significant incentive for retirement income, while not placing additional current income tax burdens on the employee. Since it is the intention of the employer to accumulate funds for the employee over an extended period, select an investment that defers the tax on the funds' earnings.

This arrangement is a *non-qualified deferred compensation plan*. The plan's purpose is to retain key people. Furthermore, it can provide partial indemnity for the company against the loss of a key person because permanent life insurance owned by the employer funds deferred compensation plans.

Insurance values become a balance sheet asset. Death proceeds that exceed payments promised to the key employee become a tax free addition to company surplus.

Finally, an important benefit is that it doesn't require Internal Revenue Service approval. An owner can choose the people he wants to participate in the plan.

There are special advantages for the key employee as well. The plan helps meet needs for retirement income planning in a measurable and effective way. It recognizes the key executive's value to the company and becomes an incentive for continued exemplary performance.

The mechanics of the plan are simple. By contract, the company agrees to pay the key employee or his beneficiary a stated sum of money over some period of years. The company funds the commitment through purchase and ownership of a permanent life insurance policy on the key employee. Although the premiums are not tax deductible when paid, the later payouts to the key employee are. Remember, the proceeds of the policy will ultimately be received income tax free by the company. (See Diagram A)

Though it is important to build equity in the business, an argument can be made for extracting a small piece of this cash equity each year and setting it aside for future uses. The same rationale holds true for the interests of your key personnel. Creating a cash position for them on the books of the company's balance sheet represents an incentive as well as a reward. And, unlike a privately-held stock incentive, it's possible to create a predetermined benefit level at a selected future date and lock it in.

Also unlike the stock incentive, it almost always results in a true wealth-creating opportunity for the key employee, and avoids the legal problems that too frequently result from privately-held minority stock ownership promises gone bad.

DIAGRAM A

Deferred Compensation Plan

```
$ $ $ $ $ $ $ $ $ $                  $ $ $ $ $ $ $ $ $ $ $
$                    $              $                      $
$ Aggressive, Inc. $- - - Premiums - - ->$   Insurance    $
$                    $              $      Company         $
$ $ $ $ $ $ $ $ $ $                  $ $ $ $ $ $ $ $ $ $ $
```

For Policy on Life of Keyperson:
Policy Values Owned by Aggressive, Inc.

At Death of Keyperson:

```
$ $ $ $ $ $ $ $ $ $
$        Insurance      $
$        Company        $   Income Tax-Free
$                       $   - - - Proceeds - - ->   $ $ $ $ $ $ $ $ $ $ $
$ $ $ $ $ $ $ $ $ $                                 $                     $
$ $ $ $ $ $ $ $ $ $      Tax Deductible            $  Aggressive, Inc. $
$                       $<- - - - Dollars - - - -   $                     $
$       Keyperson's     $                            $ $ $ $ $ $ $ $ $ $ $
$         Estate        $
$ $ $ $ $ $ $ $ $ $
```

AT RETIREMENT OF KEYPERSON:

```
$ $ $ $ $ $ $ $ $ $                  $ $ $ $ $ $ $ $ $ $ $
$                    $  Can Pay Cash  $                     $
$ Aggressive, Inc. $- - - - Values - - ->$    Keyperson    $
$                    $  (Deductible)  $                     $
$ $ $ $ $ $ $ $ $ $                  $ $ $ $ $ $ $ $ $ $ $
```

PEOPLE HABIT 9

Putting PEP (Per Employee Productivity) into Your Organization

Money is an entrepreneur's most powerful motivating tool. Properly structured, cash incentives develop people by providing performance feedback, helping employees create savings or wealth, increasing profitability and dramatically improving productivity.

I have designed and implemented two ways to increase your organization's PEP—*Per Employee Productivity*. These cash incentive concepts, an excellent alternative to privately-held stock incentives, have been in place at our magazine for more than five years. They are working well, providing a win-win situation for everyone in our organization.

Much is written about teamwork and worker productivity, but it's typically abstract theory or professorial preaching. Seldom are these ideas discussed in a practical, "This is exactly how it can be done" context.

Equity Alternative I
SSI—*The Sales Support Incentive*

Every business has two types of employees—those who bring in the revenue, the revenue producers. And those who service the revenue, the revenue supporters. One of the constant challenges in organizations with a commissioned sales force is reducing the level of natural antagonism between the commissioned sales department and the salaried support staff. At our magazine we created the Sales Support Incentive (SSI), which is producing a lively, successful team spirit. Our innovative SSI concept was recently the subject of an *Inc.* magazine story.

The purpose of SSI is to reward employees (other than commissioned sales people) for enthusiastically supporting our advertising revenue growth.

Here's how it works:

Our publishing organization has three departments in addition to sales. They are news, composition, and front office. We issued a total of 1,000 shares of SSI stock to the three departments as follows:

News 250 shares

Composition 500 shares

Front Office 250 shares

All non-sales staff members participate.

We empowered employees to negotiate the distribution of shares within their department. There haven't been any disagreements, but the general manager arbitrates the distribution of shares if the need occurs.

We calculate and pay the cash incentive monthly, based on advertising revenue pages above the base level identified when we installed the incentive. SSI is worth about $2,500 per year per employee and growing.

SSI shares are issued in fixed quantity to the department—not to the individual. In addition to promoting the spirit of teamwork, this structure encourages per employee productivity. How? The fixed number of shares dilutes each employee's interest if the department adds employees. Additions reduce each employee's percentage ownership of the dollars paid to the department where the new hire occurred. Each employee assumes the identity of the employer since a new hire costs both the employer and the employee money. SSI creates a natural desire for each employee to defer the hire as long as possible, therefore boosting per employee productivity.

SSI has rewarded everyone on our team several fold. One of the payoffs for me came last January. Our lead typesetter, who carries much of the increased composition workload of a growing magazine, told me—with a smile—to get those advertising people rolling so she could pay her Christmas bills.

That's when I knew SSI was maximizing PEP—*Per Employee Productivity*—in our organization.

Equity Alternative II
Employee Profit Ownership Plan (EPOP)

This is the second cash incentive plan we use to measure achievement and reward productivity. *Tri-State Neighbor* issues employees profit certificates that give them 10 percent ownership of the monthly pre-tax earnings, rounded to the nearest $100.

All full-time employees are eligible to participate on the first January 1 of their employment. Each employee's profit ownership is determined annually according to the following:

A. All employees who have been full-time for at least ten months receive an initial offering of 100 profit shares.

B. Each enrolled employee receives an additional five (5) shares of EPOP stock for every year of full-time employment completed as of each January 1.

C. Each employee receives one EPOP share for every thousand dollars of earnings during the previous calendar year.

D. The general manager, advertising manager, news editor, and business manager receive a 20 share Department Head Premium.

Total EPOP shares outstanding are fixed during the calendar year, changing only on January 1, as provided by the preceding four-part formula. EPOP payouts range from $3,500 to $6,000 per employee per year. In an organization with a strong emphasis on per employee productivity, EPOP should increase faster than corporate earnings.

Summary

Each month, upon completion of the profit and loss statement, the business manager and the general manager calculate and post the monthly SSI and EPOP earnings per share. SSI and EPOP payments are made monthly on the 20th of the month following.

The uniqueness of these incentive plans is their encouragement of per employee productivity. With SSI, revenue units must increase faster than the number of employees required to produce the revenue. For EPOP, pre-tax profits must increase faster than the number of shares outstanding. When these productivity goals are met, each employee's incentive paycheck increases. When staff levels grow at the same rate as output and profit, incentive payments are the same. And when the number of employees grows faster than revenue pages (SSI) or earnings (EPOP), it creates lower per-employee productivity and incentive payments to each employee decrease.

These cash incentives have created some lively discussions. During one meeting a department head indicated he was thinking of adding a new person. Before the meeting was over, other staff members had volunteered to chip in to handle the department head's need. They didn't want a marginally-needed new hire to reduce their EPOP awards.

Employee response to these two plans is highly gratifying. We all look for opportunities to build a cohesive team. That's what SSI and EPOP are doing—delivering a strong, team-oriented working environment. Awareness of personal productivity is high, and if someone forgets it, a fellow employee is likely to provide a pleasant reminder.

The Sales Support Incentive and Employee Profit Ownership Plan are two living examples of cash incentive strategies that work for everyone. Whenever we can find ways to get employees and employers on one wavelength we've got a winner. Take advantage of every such opportunity.

PEOPLE HABIT 10

Getting the Most Bang for Your Incentive Buck

"Effective incentives describe what the person gets paid to do."

Effective incentive design is an increasingly important opportunity. Obviously, we want to get the most mileage possible from our incentive awards.

There are four rules to apply when seeking to increase the motivational mileage of incentives, except those directed at the highest levels of the organization.

Effective incentives are:

1) Boldly designed.

2) Quickly paid.

3) Attention grabbing through celebration.

4) Paid in cash (be sure to treat cash payments properly for tax purposes). Optimize the impact of a boldly designed plan by scheduling payments at least monthly. Quarterly, semi-annual or annual payouts don't have the punch that monthly or more frequent payments have.

Why do incentives exist? To share and to motivate. While a dollar is a dollar, a delayed dollar greatly reduces its motivational value. On the other hand, if our associates work hard this month to get paid extra next month, they are likely to want to get out there and go for it.

Our restaurant group embarked on a mission to significantly upgrade the quality and tenure of our restaurant co-workers. We created the Cash Bonus Account, which we called CBA, and offered a dollar per hour cash bonus to each employee meeting stated criteria. Its impact was extraordinary.

I was checking into a Des Moines hotel a couple of weeks after we announced this unique and inviting incentive. When I offered my corporate credit card the night manager said, "I know you. You're the guy who pays your employees so well."

Gee, that was neat! Indeed, it was a bold effort and an unusually attractive opportunity for our people. We knew almost immediately that it would accomplish its purpose. But the kind of recognition and goodwill our organization received was a surprise bonus.

This incentive's purpose included a retention goal, so we couldn't pay it more often than quarterly. When the first quarter was over, however, we weren't timid. We loaded $38,000 into an armored car, and our vice president and general manager followed the truck to each restaurant and distributed the cash, one employee at a time. What energy we created!

It was a successful incentive, quickly serving notice that we were the market leaders when it came to treatment of co-workers. We became one of the employers of choice in Des Moines.

PEOPLE HABIT 11

Pay Fewer People More

Mark McCormack said it in *What They Don't Teach You At Harvard Business School*. Tom Peters said it in *Pursuit Of Excellence*. In case it's still a mystery, I'll say it here: One of the fundamentally important entrepreneurial opportunities is finding ways to employ fewer people and pay them more.

PEOPLE HABIT 12

Motivation in Perspective

"The starting point of all achievement is desire. Weak desires bring weak results, just as a small amount of fire makes a small amount of heat."

— *Napoleon Hill*

America is confused about motivation. We have been taken in by consultants, authors, and speakers preaching on how we need to go out and "fire up the troops." They discuss motivation as though it's a rah-rah party, led by a charismatic, effusive and entertaining leader who puts on a periodic road show to fill everyone's motivational tank. How nice it would be.

Years ago someone told me that a leader doesn't know how good he is until he leaves. That was a new perspective for me, but one I now champion. The school of thought suggesting motivation is a daily, hands-on leadership requirement has given many capable leaders migraine headaches. It's too much to ask.

Enlightened motivation is more structural than personal. It's built on trust, not a winning smile, personality, or charisma. Bringing out the best instincts in people isn't achieved at the snap

---

of the finger. It requires the development of a comfort level, delegation, adequate training, and a sense of individual importance.

Achievers succeed by developing more than businesses. They develop people to become surrogate leaders. These surrogates are more than willing to step in and "strut their stuff" at every opportunity. The surrogate knows, and others notice, when he or she has the opportunity to lead. Sometimes all we have to do is get out of the way.

Passing along the torch of responsibility is a top motivator. When you're good, periodic absences have little impact on the organization you leave behind. When the leader isn't effective, there's a need to be continuously present. It sounds backwards, but it's true. Beware the owner whose business is more than a few years old who doesn't feel comfortable leaving.

> Several years ago I was holding an annual review with an employee who had recently joined us. During his job interview he had portrayed himself as an energetic, aggressive worker from the school of hard luck.

> Two months into the job, it was obvious that something was missing in his attitude. We discussed my concerns during the review. I found the reason for his lackluster performance. Our organization distressed him because no one was motivating him.

I've been handed that "you aren't motivating me baggage" (and garbage) before. But I don't accept it. I hand it back.

The leader has a responsibility—an absolute responsibility—to create an environment within which an employee can motivate him or herself. To accomplish that, the employer-employee relationship must be founded on trust, mutual respect, and a sense of fair play. The supervisor, however, is not directly responsible to motivate each person. That's the individual's personal responsibility and opportunity.

The leader's responsibility is to be sure the organization has a properly set motivational table. Then individuals can eat with their own fork. The next time anyone in your working environment hands you their fork and asks you to feed them motivation, here are two things you should do: First, check your organization's motivational table to be sure it has adequate nourishment. If it does, then hand the fork back and suggest the employee feed him or herself.

To lead is a responsibility. To babysit is not.

PEOPLE HABIT 13

Develop with Delegation

Delegation is a way of sharing authority and responsibility. More important, it's a way to develop people.

Yielding responsibility is difficult, especially for entrepreneurs. An entrepreneur becomes highly self-reliant in the early stages of a venture when delegation is seldom an option. That fosters the habit that "if you want it done right, do it yourself."

Early entrepreneurship requires self-confidence, while delegation requires confidence in others. Delegation, in turn, provides an opportunity for employees to build their own confidence. It's a chain reaction that, in highly entrepreneurial organizations, involves all employee levels.

A beginning entrepreneurship requires establishment of a strong personal foundation. Mature entrepreneurship requires the transfer of that foundation to others. In the middle lies a continuous process of preparing successors for the day when the founder will pass the baton.

Preparing successors is difficult under the best of conditions. We can falter in several ways—by not preparing a successor, by preparing a successor too late, thereby not having enough time to *test*, or by choosing the wrong successor. Each phase of the entrepreneurial cycle is difficult, but for most entrepreneurs, providing for succession is difficult with a capital *D*.

The MBA in Delegation

To Doug Tompkins, co-founder of Esprit de Corp, MBA means *Managing by Being Away*. I like that.

Unquestionably, entrepreneurial successes are created when leaders have the courage to hand the steering wheel to prepared associates, then get out of their way. While enlightened delegation focuses on developing talent rather than reducing the founder's workload, delegation does have the clear benefit of allowing the entrepreneur to graze in other pastures. Unless retirement is closing in, the true entrepreneurial leader uses the flexibility to learn, explore, and prepare for a new frontier.

Delegation is an absolute requirement for an entrepreneurial achiever who wants to create considerable wealth and who occasionally makes an entrepreneurial mark in more than one industry. The road to that level of entrepreneurial contribution has only one route, a route that travels through delegation.

Here are eight necessary steps in effective transitional delegation:

1. *Prepare a strategic plan annually*. It contains the organization's guidelines, goals, and objectives for the coming year. The plan should specify who is responsible for what, and on what date.

2. *Be accessible*. The new leader needs the comfort of knowing you're available when needed.

3. *Broaden the feeling of ownership*. References like *my* company are inappropriate. The most desirable type of ownership is the pride of *feeling* like an owner, and is created through empowerment.

4. *Endow the new leader with at least as much authority as responsibility*.

5. *Create pay incentives that match the job description*. Tie compensation incentives and the job description so closely together that it's obvious how the new leader is paid and what is expected.

6. *Coach and counsel*. Prepare your observations and discuss them one on one. Allow for differences in the new leader's approach.

7. *Be publicly supportive.* Reinforce the new leader's impact with the group.

8. *Be gone part of the time.* Become involved in new interests, expand your horizons (maybe even go the mountains in Colorado and write a book). Renew the entrepreneurial juices while letting the new leader run the show without you.

PEOPLE HABIT 14

Delegation: The Master Manager of Time

In the previous Habit, we approached delegation from the perspective of developing people. The art of delegation, however, has multiple payoffs. Beyond growing and empowering people, delegation is a profoundly important tool for personal productivity.

One of America's most popular seminar topics is time management. Affiliates of Leadership Management, Inc. offer one of many time management programs. It is authored by founder Paul J. Meyer.

In his Effective Time Management course, Meyer devotes one of six weekly lessons to the time management benefits of delegating. Calling delegation the "one master strategy" for managing time effectively, he credits delegation with freeing leaders at all levels to make decisions, plan, dream, or visualize new opportunities. He also suggests that delegation requires the leader to plan the amount of freedom each subordinate should have. He breaks delegation into five levels.

Level 1.　*Wait until told.* This lowest level of delegation involves the worker who performs only routine activities and only when told. Assembly line workers are examples.

Level 2.　*Seek direction, then approval.* Workers at this level bring all matters to you for instruction excepting the

---

routine. Work completed at this level is immediately returned to the supervisor for approval.

Level 3.   *Seek approval, then act.* One at this level of delegation brings problems to the supervisor with suggested solutions. The supervisor approves or disapproves the suggestions and the worker acts within this framework.

Level 4.   *Act and report immediately.* The employee makes the decision but informs the supervisor immediately of any action taken outside established guidelines. Any mistake can be corrected quickly before damage is done.

Level 5.   *Act and report routinely.* This level of delegation is reserved for competent, trained, and highly dependable people. This level requires only routine interval reporting. While initially taking the most time to set up parameters, it produces the biggest payoff in time saved by the supervisor or leader.

PEOPLE HABIT 15

When Responsibility Is a Dirty Word, Someone Lacks Authority

Everyone likes authority. Achievers like responsibility. My brief "big company" experience introduced me to the world of responsibility without authority. It's not a comfortable place to be. Yet people are put there routinely.

Responsibility without authority is the work of either a manipulator of people or an unenlightened delegator. It is patently unfair because the person with the delegated responsibility absorbs the blame—while the one with the authority takes the credit. The employee is in a no-win situation.

The first rule of delegation is—never assign responsibility without providing at least equal authority. Every empowered employee in America shares *at least* one common trait—he or she always has at least as much authority to act as responsibility to perform.

Associates who care about their work and are good at what they do enrich my entrepreneurial life. I try to delegate to these future leaders in a way that is ethical, fair, and thoughtful. Legitimate control must accompany responsibility. When it doesn't, everyone loses.

PEOPLE HABIT 16

Participation Doesn't Mean Democracy

I believe in participative management. I have a hunch, however, that I define it differently than many others.

Participative management was a buzz-word in the '70s and early '80s. To some, it meant calling a staff meeting now and then and getting some ideas. Others thought it meant "management by committee." Still others related to it as a way to be *humanistic*. On the fringe were those who interpreted it to mean one-person, one-vote democracy.

I called a meeting of our publishing staff to involve my associates in an important decision. It related to the long-term positioning of our publication.

The *Tri-State Neighbor* was almost six years old. Since day one, we referred to it as a regional newspaper. More and more, however, our national advertisers, and even our readers, were using *magazine* when talking about us. That was understandable. We had many of the graphic and distribution qualities of a magazine, and most of our peers across the country called themselves magazines. Although internally we used the newspaper reference, the increasing usage of *magazine* from the outside was causing a gradual but growing internal uncertainty about our identity and position in the marketplace.

During the meeting I shared my concern that we were becoming increasingly confused about our identity. A lengthy discussion followed, with excellent give and take. The meeting ended with a majority view that we should remain a newspaper. And that's what we did.

Three months later, I called another meeting on the repositioning topic. The magazine references were continuing to grow. I felt something had to be done before we became even more uncertain about our identity. At that meeting I shared my growing concerns, indicating that something should be done to put us on a more defined road to our future. I asked my associates, with a sense of urgency, to join me in moving our stated market position from newspaper to magazine. There was general understanding, although not total agreement, with my conclusions. We repositioned as a magazine.

There are times when leaders must lead. This was such a time. I felt strongly that our identity needed redefinition. I sensed it was important we set out together on a more assured and visible course. I concluded that the dominant risk was *doing nothing*. Participative management is good, but thoughtful leadership is no less important in the participative environment.

PEOPLE HABIT 17

I Thought You Would Never Ask

Can you help me?

May I have your assistance in understanding this?

Will you give me your opinion?

What do you think?

Many view asking a question as a weakness, a sign of inadequacy. To the achiever, it's a way to learn and grow. Feeling comfortable asking questions is one of the habits that achievers regularly practice. It's a definite sign of strength.

Asking questions is a great way to get closer to someone. Inquiry nurtures relationships. Since the more self-confident individual usually does the asking, it can add balance to a relationship by offering the less confident participant an opportunity to answer the question—and feel important.

Sustained inquiry is the habit of an alert, engaged mind. It's something that successful people do. Achievers have an endless appetite to expand knowledge, an insatiable desire to learn.

Lack of knowledge is not our major risk. Fooling ourselves into thinking we know enough, thereby abandoning the process of discovery, is our major hazard. Achieving entrepreneurship, by definition, doesn't exist without inquisitiveness.

Leaders inquire to feed their souls, to stay abreast of today and become acquainted with tomorrow. But they also probe on behalf of their organizations. Organizations achieve through the leader's knowledge.

Inquisitive leaders create a learning environment. When the leader asks questions, others feel free to do likewise. The net result is better communication, more give and take, and a workplace more alive with learning and contemplation.

More basically, inquisitiveness is required for survival. The knowledge gained moves organizations forward. Habitual inquisitiveness tunes skills, allowing achievers to gather knowledge at a rate far beyond the competition.

Another trait of inquisitive people is mental flexibility. New knowledge updates and replaces the old, purging obsolete beliefs and references. This constant updating helps keep an achieving entrepreneur ahead of the pack.

Yet another value of asking a question is creating an opportunity to listen. When listening, avoid the trap of anticipating what others will say. Listen between the lines.

Often, what's said doesn't reveal nearly as much as what isn't said. Good listeners can also act ignorant, creating increased trust while diffusing the "I know it all" apprehensions.

Those who inquire have the most opportunity to listen. Those who listen have the most opportunity to learn. Those who learn have the most current knowledge. And knowledge is money. Thus the importance of asking questions.

PEOPLE HABIT 18

A Little Thought Will Say a Lot

A short "thank you" or "I noticed your accomplishments" note is a powerful way to give positive reinforcement to a friend, customer, associate, or relative.

In a world where compliments are far too few, you have the potential to stand above the crowd by acknowledging effort and achievement.

Big people are note senders. They actively cheer for others, celebrating occasions of achievement whenever possible. Notes can be typed or handwritten. That's a matter of style. More important is that you care about the achievements and contributions of others and are willing to communicate your congratulations and good feelings.

Be a *big* person. Don't hesitate to congratulate.

PEOPLE HABIT 19

Introduction First, Name Second

Do you find yourself not listening attentively during an introduction to a new acquaintance? I sure do. And it happens to others when they're introduced to me, especially since I have two one-syllable names.

To help others remember who I am, I've changed my style. Rather than saying "I'm Bill Byrne, glad to meet you, Jenny," I hitch my name to the back. "It's nice to meet you, Jenny. My name is Bill Byrne." It's different and allows more time to get the other party's attention before I say what I really want remembered—my name.

PEOPLE HABIT 20

Give a Warm, Two-Handed Handshake

A friend and her family were having a party in celebration of her recent law degree. A lady I hadn't seen for a long time walked up and gave me one of the warmest handshakes I've received in a long time. While shaking right hands, she put her left hand on my right forearm. There's nothing new about it, but few do it as enthusiastically as she did.

Her handshake made such an impression that we started talking about the various ways people shake hands. She related that the handshake she gave me was the "Dolly Madison handshake." That was the first time I'd known a handshake to have a name.

A warm handshake makes a marvelous impression. Give an enthusiastic *Dolly Madison* the next time you want to leave a strong impression.

V

ACHIEVING THROUGH CUSTOMER RELATIONSHIPS

"Anybody who thinks customers aren't important should try doing without them for ninety days."

Developing positive, professional relationships isn't difficult. All that's required is keeping our heart in the right place. We need to understand above all that others have expectations of us that we must diligently live up to. Effective relationships in our professional lives are achievable by simply doing a few things very, very well.

This chapter discusses some of the basic relationship-building habits professional people practice and identifies three distinct levels of customer service.

CUSTOMER HABIT 1

Using Your Customer's Most Prized Possession to Your Advantage

Associates like it when I say it. So do friends. And customers feel good when we say it, whether they're in our office or on the telephone. What is it?

It's our most prized possession. It's our name. One of the simplest, yet most valuable keys to developing successful and warm customer relationships is having everyone in your organization use names. The first name is almost always safe to use, and it's warmer and friendlier than the Mr., Ms., or Mrs.

I recently spent an hour with Bill McGrane, one of America's foremost experts on self-esteem. I asked him to share some of the ways we can make others feel good.

His first comment was, "Call them by name five times every time you talk with them, and do it as soon in the conversation as possible."

Whether on the telephone or in person, everyone in your organization has the power to make others feel good. Learn names and use them faithfully and frequently.

CUSTOMER HABIT 2

Don't Treat New Customers Better than Old Ones

We're always reaching for the new customer. We really need to reach equally hard to satisfy the old ones.

Our restaurant group has been doing business with a major supplier for more than 10 years. Our account is important to them, as we were their first sizable restaurant customer. In 1989, they began supplying the operator of a similar restaurant in a nearby city. The new customer represented less than 20 percent of our volume, yet to get the new business they priced their product almost five percent less than what we were paying.

Their behavior was both unfair and unethical. The opportunity, in this case study, is to understand that *fairness requires treating all similar customers similarly*. It's not only unfair, it's stupid to play the kind of pricing game this supplier did. How would you feel if you were one of their loyal customers?

This example might appear preposterous, but businesses do it all the time. Can you imagine being a long-time customer and finding out the man or woman down the street is getting a better price for the same or less volume?

A company I've done business with for many years is well-intended, but sometimes ethically misguided. For years, they've made policy exceptions—a bad case of greasing the squeaky wheel. If a sales rep does something not in compliance with their policy, they look the other way. If a customer can't or won't pay certain charges, they aren't attentive to collecting. And so the story goes.

From their point of view, they are being lenient and forgiving. In reality, however, they are being patently unfair. They are asking, even requiring, standards from some—but not from all. They make arbitrary exceptions, yet require others to tow the line. What's fair about that? Not much.

Treating customers fairly means all similar customers are treated similarly. Any time you make an exception for one, you put every other similar customer at an unfair disadvantage.

Offering promotional deals is fine. But make them available to everyone. You owe that fairness to all customers, all the time.

CUSTOMER HABIT 3

Reality Isn't Real.
Expectations Are.

I'm away from home more than I like. I prefer driving if my trip is short and time permits. Driving allows additional control over my schedule, I can dictate notes, and it provides a chance to exceed expectations.

For years, when returning home by car, I've given my wife, Lynne, a bogus arrival time. Usually, I'll say nine if I think I'll be there at eight, midnight if it looks like eleven, etc. And I do the same after a golf game or meeting.

There's only one reason I do it—to be sure I live up to Lynne's expectations.

If I say I'm going to be back in town at ten, for example, and return at eleven, I've disappointed her. On the other hand, if I say midnight and return at eleven she's appreciative of my promptness. What changed? I returned at eleven o'clock in both examples. Which situation is better for our relationship? It's obvious.

When world leaders meet to reduce arms we really don't evaluate their success on the basis of how many missiles they agree to eliminate. We reach our conclusions from how the press plays it versus expectations. They could reduce missiles by 100,000 and we would be disappointed if our expectations were higher. Or they could reduce by 50,000 and we would be ecstatic if we anticipated nothing. Perceptions. Expectations. Not reality.

Customers rate our performance the same way. If we say we're going to do something, we had better do it. And on time. Many of us overlook this simple opportunity to please others. When you have confidence that there's a deadline or goal you can meet, put it on the record and produce. If you're going to perform the task on time, you should position yourself to get maximum credit for it.

Several years ago we did all our laundry and cleaning business with the place closest to our home. Time after time they told us our clothes would be ready "tomorrow at three." They were—about half the time.

We weren't happy customers and eventually took our business elsewhere. The new cleaners promised us "tomorrow at four." They never missed. And we were happy customers.

The first cleaners thought our clothes might be ready by three and committed to it. The smarter cleaners was probably sure they would also have them ready by three, but they told us four, reducing the risk of disappointment. Our perception was that one really had it together, while the other didn't know what they were doing. Probably too harsh, but that was our perception.

At the core of your customer, professional, and personal relationships is your willingness to make and keep commitments. If you can keep a promise, make one. If not, promise nothing.

We turn customers off when we take our commitments too casually. We also turn off our employees. In one moment with a loose tongue we can promise something to an employee that will haunt our credibility for years. Again, a promise loosely made is a promise easily forgotten. It takes a toll in many, many businesses.

Most of the obstacles we face are difficult to solve. This one isn't. If you make a promise to someone, keep it. If you can't, let them know before you default and tell them why. They will understand and give you another chance.

This is very important. Much of the impression you make on someone depends on how well you deliver on the expectations others have of you. Businesses have both failed and succeeded because of performance vs. expectations. Don't blow it!

CUSTOMER HABIT 4

Completing the Communication Loop Is a 360 Degree Commitment

View effective communication as a series of contacts organized to:

1) Make the other party feel good about him or herself.

2) Make the other party feel good about me.

3) Complete the task to everyone's satisfaction.

Some business communication requires only a singular activity—meaning one letter, one telephone conversation, or one face to face conversation takes care of everything. The more important the communication, however, the greater the likelihood that it will require multiple contacts to complete the objective. I propose my thoughts on effective communication in the context of the latter example—when it requires more than one interface.

Picture communication as a 360 degree loop with the initial contact beginning at the top of the circle. Before you complete the communication you must travel the entire 360 degrees in stages, one contact at a time, back to the top of the loop. The completion of the communication loop occurs only when the needs and expectations of both parties are satisfied.

Effective communication is, like other aspects of business life, a matter of expectation. Did you call the person back if you received a message to do so? Did you do it within their time expectations? Did you put the letter you promised in the mail, and did you do it on time? Did you perform all requested or promised follow up on a timely basis? In other words, did you perform as the other party expected?

Communicating with the needs and desires of the other party in mind is a courtesy. It is also a self-imposed requirement of professional people.

The biggest challenge I face in closing the communication loop occurs when I'm away. Even then, if my office views it as important or if it's important to the other party, I get a fax and respond within 24 hours.

Another opportunity to complete the communication loop is to return every phone call. With three business listings in the phone book I have triple the fun with solicitors and other unavoidable interruptions. Nonetheless, if someone asks me to return a call, I do. Period. I may not feel a need to talk with the caller, but he or she wants to talk with me. That's good enough. Professional courtesy requires I complete the communication loop. And I do.

Think about the communication loop. Do you go the full 360 degrees to respond to the needs, desires, or expectations of the other party? Do you accomplish the three items suggested at the top of this Habit? Do you do your part to make other people feel good about themselves and about you? Do you complete the objective to everyone's satisfaction?

Professionalism requires you close the communication loop every time it's opened.

CUSTOMER HABIT 5

Scoring Customer Points with Telephone Manners

I dial a number. A voice answers, "Mountain Pine Company."

"Is John there?" I ask.

"May I tell him who's calling?"

"This is Bill Byrne."

"One moment, please." After holding a minute, Miss Manners comes back to the phone.

"I'm sorry, John can't come to the phone right now. May I have him call you?"

I say, "Thank you, I'll call back later."

What just happened? Was John in a meeting? Or didn't John want to talk with me? I don't know the answer. This scenario leaves me with uncertainty as to why John wouldn't come to the phone. It offends me.

It offends me because, for whatever reason, John didn't come to the phone after he knew who was calling. I just received a telephone rebuff I took personally. It's OK if John really couldn't take the call. But he knew it was me, and maybe he just chose not to answer. How do I know the difference?

The "May I ask who's calling" syndrome is telephone manners at its worst.

Getting the caller's name is more often a method to support self-importance than necessary call screening. In my experience, important people don't ask who is calling. They pick up the phone and away we go.

Our telephone answerers at The Byrne Companies don't ask who is calling except in the most unusual circumstances. We expect everyone in our organization to be fully accessible to all callers. No games—no ego-building.

Poor telephone manners are amplified by using the above verbal gymnastics, then picking up the phone without acknowledging the caller's identity. Why in the world would you ask for a name and then be so self-important you don't acknowledge it when you answer? The caller's most important possession is his or her name. Use it!

One way I could have taken the leadership in diffusing this problem is to have removed the need for the "Who's calling" question by giving my name. "Good morning, this is Bill Byrne. Is John in?" The game's over before it starts, and many receptionists no doubt appreciate the courtesy.

Good leaders have a distinct preference to reduce barriers. It may be an open door or an open telephone. Aloofness and inaccessibility are as negative on the telephone as in person. The payoff of "May I tell him who's calling" is minimal while the risk to personal and customer relationships is considerable. Consider how your telephone manners impact the caller's feelings. Remove the barriers.

CUSTOMER HABIT 6

Creating the Delighted Customer

The current *buzz* topic in business and on the speaking circuit is how a business can continuously and effectively reinforce customer relationships. Generally, this activity is called customer service.

The term customer service is incomplete, failing to communicate the depth of the relationship that excellent organizations develop with customers. Moreover, customer service is a self-perception, a view of how the business thinks it's serving the customer. Indeed, the business may perceive the customer as well-served, but so what? It means nothing if the customer disagrees.

We shouldn't confuse customer service with service effectiveness. When we get our report card, our customer won't define the relationship's strength by how well we *serve* but how effectively we helped them in reaching their objectives. In other words, our customer *style* can be terrific, but we may still flunk the effectiveness test if we're not offering the *substance* needed to meet needs or expectations.

Winning and keeping customers requires we provide value that propels the customer's life forward. That's good cause to elevate our thinking from providing mere customer service to the next higher level, *customer satisfaction*. At this level, the customer relationship focuses on the perspective of the customer, not the provider.

While customer satisfaction is customer-defined and represents a level of customer relationship that's praiseworthy, there's an even higher level of performance that wealth-building entrepreneurial achievers seek. I call it *customer delight.*

When customers are served, providers fulfill their own expectations. When customers are *satisfied*, customer expectations are fulfilled. However, when providers exceed expectation, they *delight* customers. Delighted customers become proactive supporters, our vocal cheerleaders. They become "employed customers," members of the team.

Since 1983 I've collected thoughts that I call Customer Commandments. They create customer loyalty and delight. Here they are:

1. *Stay close to your customers.* Sales people too often lose touch. Stay close. Don't contact a customer only when you have something to sell. Visit in person or by phone at other times when your purpose is simply to reinforce the relationship. Share a piece of pertinent information or just check to be sure all is going as planned. Practice the *sales-stutter*—one call to sell, then one to satisfy, then another to sell, etc. A non-selling contact is important to the health of a delighted customer relationship.

2. *The most important customer is the existing customer.* We become so charged up opening new accounts we too often forget to serve delightfully those most important to us.

   A couple of years ago I encouraged a friend to open an account at a different bank. He did. Recently, another friend of his, who had been a customer of the bank for more than 25 years, found out the bank offered his new customer friend an interest-bearing checking account. The customer of 25 years hadn't been offered the same opportunity. Irritated by this omission, he changed banks.

   It doesn't pay to build a business on the backs of your existing, loyal customers. Make your deals available to all customers—not just new ones.

Bill Byrne

3. *Don't advertise—surprise.* You don't develop relationships with delightfully satisfied customers with fanfare and promotion, but with action.

   Advertising stimulates business by promising a lot, then often delivering less than promised. A delighted customer results when we determine what the customer needs, promise it, then deliver more than promised.

   We're besieged by advertising promises. When it comes to the delightfully satisfied customer, however, there is no room for advertising hype. What counts is delivery. Effective organizations don't overpromise when forming their delighted customer strategy. But they do *overdeliver.*

4. *Be genuine.* The delightfully satisfied customer can only be served by someone genuinely wanting to help. Someone focused more on the needs of the customer than his own. Genuine, caring people are givers, and in giving they achieve—for themselves, their customers, and their organization.

5. *Customer delight begins during the sale.* The signing of the agreement or writing the check doesn't end the sale. That's when the sale begins. The customer's lasting impression begins during the sale and is molded after the sale. Follow up by phone, letter, note and inquiry are critical to developing repeat business—and a delighted customer.

6. *Pretend you're going to lose every customer.* Imagine the positive energy put into customer delight when we assume we are at risk of losing every customer after every sale. That assumption will motivate us to delight our customers.

7. *Promises are made to be kept.* Making promises is easy. Keeping them isn't. The number of promises we make is less important than the number we keep. Relationships are built on expectations. It's far worse to make a promise and not keep it than not to have promised at all. Don't disappoint.

8. *Plan your style.* The successful entrepreneurial organization invests time in planning. Delivering customer delight requires a planned, unique style that has the potential to become a visible service trademark.

9. *Anticipate customer needs.* Demographics, which suggest who is buying, and psychographics, which tells why they are buying, are constantly changing. Anticipating the needs of tomorrow's delighted customer requires an insight into these market characteristics, as well as a willingness to change. Strategic planning and continuous customer inquiry are opportunities effective leaders use to gain access to the leading edge of market trends.

    In the late '20s and early '30s, General Motors Chairman Alfred P. Sloan spent much of his time visiting dealers, sometimes as many as two dozen a week, getting a firsthand look at how and to whom GM cars were being sold.
    Sloan was able to re-energize General Motors by staying close to dealers and customers, a process that served as the stepping stone to a new level of market dominance by GM.
    Meanwhile, Ford was offering "any color as long as it's black" and lost considerable market share. All because Sloan, through inquiry, was able to anticipate customer needs.

10. *Creating delight is unconditional.* We can't choose the circumstances we wish to exist when delivering customer delight. There are times when creating a delighted customer will come at great cost—even an unprofitable transaction. Nonetheless, our commitment must be uninterrupted by convenience or short-term profit consideration.

11. *Customer delight begins and ends with employees.* It's a chain reaction. Extraordinary customer relationships result from extraordinary commitment to the employee. In turn,

the employee commits to the delight of the customer. Only delighted employees create delighted customers.

12. *Empower the employee.* The employee closest to the customer creates customer delight. The person on the firing line is key. The employee closest to the customer must have the authority to do whatever is necessary to provide customer delight. Throw out the wordy manuals and guidelines. They don't allow enough flexibility. Creating customer delight is intuitive, relying on the individual interacting with the customer to make the call on the spot.

    Empower employees on the front line—those answering the phone, working the delivery dock, and tending the sales desk—to anticipate and respond to customer wants. Check the length of your customer delight leash. Give the employee enough room and flexibility to create the delightfully satisfied customer.

13. *Customer delight requires a good product or service.* Many organizations have a habit of cutting corners, believing they're still capable of building strong customer relationships. It's a delusion.

    Customer delight isn't a game of trickery—it comes from the heart. It must represent the genuine, underlying integrity of the organization, fully supported by quality.

14. *Customer delight requires not only the right intent, but the right words.* We often choose harsh words when dealing with customer complaints. "You should" is better stated as "Would you consider" or "May I suggest." "Let me check" is better phrased as "May I check for you," etc. Work with your staff to determine the proper words to use in response to customer inquiries and complaints. Every telephone call, every customer interaction is handled more effectively when we choose the right word or phrase.

15. *Protect customer productivity.* A while back a traveling sales representative had a unique electrical problem with her car that required a part the dealer didn't have in stock. She had a 500 mile trip with several appointments scheduled and

needed transportation. Unfortunately, the dealer she bought the car from would provide a loaner only at significant cost.

A competing dealer responded to my request to help her. He provided an adequate car for her two day trip at minimal cost. He also gained a customer. She has since bought two new cars and a 4X4 truck from him, all because he helped her to maintain her schedule and productivity.

Our focus on customer needs is most appreciated when the customer uses our product or service to make a living. That's when we make our strongest and most delightful customer impression.

16. *Develop specific response parameters.* We need to measure customer delight. How will you know when employees achieve their customer delight goals? How will you respond to their successes? Written, objective measurements are critical to continuing excellence. Go one step further by designing incentives based on customer delight performance.

Sometimes we meet our customer's needs but not within acceptable time limits. Provide the resolution immediately if possible. Institute a sunset policy requiring same-day response. If you can't find a solution on a same-day basis, at least call back before the day is over to give your customer an update and to communicate that you're working urgently to solve the problem. *The key: respond in minutes when it takes others hours or days.*

17. *Every contributor in the customer delight chain should have the occasional, yet planned opportunity to meet the customer.* Achieving customer delight is a team sport. Accounting, reception, shipping—everyone involved in customer delight is on the team. Provide the customer an opportunity to meet these people when the customer visits your office. Better yet, ask the various participants in your customer delight chain to accompany the salesperson to visit the customer on his or her own turf. Your employees will appreciate the opportunity as much as the customer.

18. *Reach for customer feelings.* When you sense a strain in a customer relationship be proactive and initiate healing. Personalize your approach by sharing your personal concern for their account. Communicate some new ideas or approaches you think may work for them.

   Anticipating a customer's feelings is highly effective. Do it with a focus on the customer's needs, not your own. You'll find it's a wonderful tool for improving the quality of your customer relationship.

19. *Call the customer by name.* This suggestion appears more than once in this book. That's not an accident. Using a customer's name is an absolute winner. And it's easy.

   A recent hospitality survey by SRI/Gallup showed that greeting customers by name and discounting prices are the two most effective ways of building traffic from existing retail patrons. This, of course, assumes the customer likes the establishment. Moreover, when the service offered was outstanding in nature, the use of customer names proved more effective for building frequency than discounting. Use the customer's name as early in the exchange as possible. It is a sure-fire way to establish rapport and good feeling.

20. *Growth creates growth.* We must provide satisfaction, happiness, wealth, or self-image to have a delighted customer. We will achieve success by offering a product or service that meets needs in an extraordinary way. When that occurs, customer delight is possible. When it doesn't, it isn't.

21. *Customer first, employee second, profit third, community fourth.* This is the priority sequence of a business tightly focused on customer delight. The business leader is the customer delight choreographer. The employee is the dancer, interfacing with the audience during each performance. Customer delight can't occur without the employee's personal caring and warmth.

   Meeting the needs of customer and employee positions the organization to meet another need—profit. Maximized profit occurs concurrently with maximized customer relationships. Here the customer delight opportunity comes full circle. The employee executes our focus on delightful customer satisfaction, the delightfully satisfied customer provides the opportunity for higher profit and the profit provides the potential for financial benefit to the employee. All these positive forces merge to offer support to the community where the participants live and work.

The delightfully satisfied customer is the hub of a multi-spoked wheel that rolls merrily along, picking up new friends along its path.

22. *Delightful customer satisfaction is personal.* It isn't simultaneously extended to the masses, but to one individual at a time. The customer you're serving now is the one you should concentrate on. Take maximum advantage of the opportunity.

23. *Delightful satisfaction requires flexibility.* Since the "delightful feeling" is highly personal, what pleases one customer may not thrill the next. Delivering this feeling requires a supple, athletic flexibility adaptable to each situation. Bend with the need. Agility and adaptability, combined with sincere effort, create optimum results.

24. *Require accountability.* All members of the customer delight chain should thoroughly understand their role. They need to be aware of their accountability and be well rehearsed on response parameters.

25. *A delightfully satisfied customer is an appreciated customer.* Here are seven everyday ways to show appreciation to your customers:

    1. *Care.* Really, honestly care about their success and concerns.

    2. *Give.* I'm not talking price concession. Give of yourself and approach your customer relationships unselfishly. Your personal attentiveness is what the customer appreciates most.

3. *Listen.* The shortest distance between two communicators is active listening. Be the listener.

4. *Smile.* An effective way to dress up a telephone conversation is to smile while you talk. The difference it makes in how you sound is amazing. And, of course, the same goes for smiling in person.

5. *Compliment.* Compliments create magic feelings. Actively look for ways to fill your customer's emotional cup. Always look for achievements to recognize. Don't let personal and professional accomplishments go unnoticed. You can make a significant difference by looking for opportunities to pass along a compliment.

6. *Recognize.* Acknowledge your customers by name every time you come into contact with them. Nothing you say sounds better to the listener than his or her name.

7. *Try.* The customer knows when you bust your pick. If you really try, your effort to create customer delight will be appreciated.

CUSTOMER HABIT 7

A Company Is Known by the Customers It Keeps

Several years ago I filed a sheet of paper with the above title. It contained 10 customer goals. I don't remember the source, so I'll pass them along without credit.

Our First Customer Goal Is to Keep Our Customers.

Our Second Customer Goal Is to Keep Them Happy with Services and Products.

Our Third Customer Goal Is to Contribute to Our Customers' Prosperity So that We in Turn May Enjoy Prosperity.

Our Fourth Customer Goal Is to Insure that Our Customers and the General Public Think Well and Speak Well of Us.

Our Fifth Customer Goal Is to Help Attract New Customers and to Keep and Satisfy Them, Too.

Bill Byrne

**Our Sixth Customer Goal Is to Maintain
Good Communications with Our Customers
at All Times.**

**Our Seventh Customer Goal Is to Realize
that Every Customer Who Complains Is Doing
Us a Favor and Should Be Afforded Every Courtesy.**

**Our Eighth Customer Goal Is to Act
Fairly and Promptly to Resolve Complaints—
and to Build Better and More Lasting Relationships
with Our Customers when We Do.**

**Our Ninth Customer Goal Is to Make
Customer Service and Effective Complaint Handling
a Company-Wide Responsibility,
Involving All Departments and All Personnel.**

**Our Tenth Customer Goal Is to Be Known
As the Company that Keeps Its Customers
Because It Treats Them So Well.**

VI

ACHIEVING THROUGH THE ORGANIZATION

"Tomorrow's business leader, it is clear, will have to be able to organize for entrepreneurship . . . will have to know how to anticipate innovation and how to make innovation economically effective."
— *Peter Drucker*

Why do some organizations thrive while others barely survive? What is the difference between success and failure? Why are certain businesses achieving while similar companies are struggling to keep their doors open? To the serious observer of achievement and leadership, the common thread of success presents itself in vivacious, living color. Success reflects the quality of the organizational leader, the person directing the business symphony.

In 1960, Theodore Levitt wrote in his essay, *Marketing Myopia*, that the difference between significant growth and little growth was the perspective and ability of the leader. That was more than 30 years ago. Not much has changed. The lead entrepreneurial

---

achiever (there is seldom more than one early in an organization's life) shapes an environment attractive to talented people. The talent is encouraged to come forth with innovative and experimental ideas—to foster new thoughts and concepts, to challenge the status quo. Simply put, the leader encourages innovation and imagination.

We can determine if an organization has creative leadership through observation. Is it hierarchical or decentralized? Is attracting and accommodating talent a continual process? Is self-improvement encouraged? Does the organization try to bring opportunities on the horizon into focus? Does it adjust quickly to external influences? And, finally, is it customer-focused, practicing "customer closeness" actively, aggressively and constantly? All of these are "acid test" questions for an organization striving to be entrepreneurial and forward-looking. Achieving organizations answer these questions with a resounding "yes."

ORGANIZATION HABIT 1

The Top Twelve Human Characteristics of Organizations Bill Byrne Wants to Build

1. *The Organization Focuses On Excellence.* Excellence results from the practiced application of talent. Organizations, like people, are prisoners of habit—that which is done repeatedly. Excellence requires constant dissatisfaction with current conditions and perpetual reaching for something better. Excellence is not accidental. It occurs only in organizations that expect it and plan for it. The adage from Ben Hogan that only "Perfect practice makes perfect" also applies to planning. Planning is perfect practice, an organized, systematic, and continual effort that enables an individual or group to practice what it wants to become. Planning provides goals and objectives to serve as a road map. These goals and objectives are transformed into expectations, which in turn form the foundation of excellence.

2. *The Organization Selects Talent Effectively.* A key component of every achieving organization is its talent-selecting process. Sequenced interviewing, testing of basic skills, and professional, validated profiling of mental aptitudes and

personality characteristics are all increasingly important pieces in the human resources puzzle.

The leading organizations reduce selection risk by matching the job to the talent, rather than the more common practice of matching talent to the job. This results in fewer misplaced workers, increased productivity, and reduced turnover.

In most organizations selection means hiring. In achieving organizations, it's a continuing evaluation process that includes building a base of knowledge that facilitates reviewing, coaching, and selection for promotion.

3. *The Organization Is Busy.* What do most employees favor? Do they want an environment with no challenge, where little is asked of them, where they can be lazy? Or do they prefer an environment where challenge is present, where others have high expectations of them, where they work hard? The cynics pick the former. Note, however, cynics aren't leaders.

People rise to expectations. They respond to the call for action. They want an opportunity to *strut their stuff* in front of an admiring audience. And they want to be in a working group which creates the organizational success that provides them an opportunity for personal satisfaction and growth.

In a previous chapter I discussed the benefits of high PEP (Per Employee Productivity). Paying fewer people more, better positioning everyone to reach for their potential, is a formidable weapon used by achieving organizations.

4. *The Organization Cares.* Caring comes from the inside. It's real, not positioned. A caring attitude runs freely within a caring organization's veins. Caring can't be manipulated.

A caring organization may say no, disappoint, and terminate, but it does so with sensitivity and professionalism.

5. *The Organization Measures Effectively.* To measure effectively means having a system in place that is sufficiently objective to permit two or more observers to reach the same conclusion independently. Effective measurement is an

unemotional process that gauges the person's work. Ineffective measurement gauges the person.

6. *The Organization Enhances Relationships.* It develops opportunities to build teamwork and a common identity of purpose within the group. It creates informal partnerships between employees and departments, and between employee and employer.

   This only occurs when everyone understands, through planning, where the organization wants to go. Without that knowledge, the team tries to pull the corporate wagon in different directions.

7. *The Organization Distributes Choices.* Responsibility is decentralized. People are aware of what is to be done and comfortable that they have adequate latitude to do it.

   Distributing choices offers significant potential for developing excellence in customer relationships, giving the employee closest to the customer more responsibility and authority to create *customer delight.* Organizations with delighted customers allow the employee on the firing line greater discretion to do what's needed to accommodate customers.

   Organizations which distribute choices effectively have a horizontal structure with less hierarchy and less distance between the top and bottom of the organizational chart. While the leader is prominent in creating the organization's strategy and focus, it's the empowered entrepreneurial associate who implements and executes the agreed upon strategy.

8. *The Organization Is Highly Ethical.* The leader sets the pace. Honesty, integrity, and a visible sense of fairness give assurance to employees and customers that a well-defined ethical boundary is at the heart of the organization.

9. *The Organization Encourages Experimentation.* Achieving organizations believe the status quo is no go, that without change there is no future.

Experimentation is not a science. It's an art form requiring accommodation of mistakes, false starts, and failure. Every organization and every person has the potential to do better. Organizations that encourage experimentation perform more to their potential and enrich the lives of their people, then give employees the opportunity to be wrong while they reach.

10. *The Organization Shares Success.* An entrepreneurial leader is, more than most others, driven to succeed. That success, however, is not egotistical or selfish. Leaders and entrepreneurial achievers refer to success as *our* rather than *my*, the company as *our* rather than *my*. As an alternative to "I did it," they say, "We did it."

Sharing includes a distribution of the benefits of success. Making employees "profitholders" is sharing. Enriching employee lives through flexible scheduling is sharing, and empowering them to lead is a way of sharing success.

Profit is a friendly, positive word in sharing environments; a nasty word in selfish ones. Staff attitudes toward profit are a ready indicator of whether or not they believe they work in a sharing organization.

A sharing company is fair. It's a feeling, not a fooling, company. It's not about big titles, calling employees partners or associates, or being humanistic. It's not about cliches. Either you are a sharing organization or you're not; either you are good to your people or you aren't. Sharing is not fancy—just authentic.

11. *The Organization Treats Employees the Way I Wanted to Be Treated when I Was An Employee.* Reflect on what was important to you as an employee. Can you reconcile that with your actions and attitudes as a leader? Are you comfortable with yourself? If not, better make some changes. But be sure you change for the right reason. Change because you have come to understand that your leadership style impacts employee performance and productivity. And performance and productivity impact profit.

12. *The Organization Promotes Lifelong Learning.* Unfortunately, I didn't become interested in learning until after I left school. Now I hunger for new thoughts, new ideas and new concepts.

One characteristic of this decade's leading organizations will be their support and encouragement of continuous training. In the 1980s American enterprise spent about one percent of payroll on training. This decade we'll spend at least two percent. The accelerated pace of professional learning results from the accelerated pace of change, combined with the decline of American education as a preparer of people.

I have read, for example, that those of us in leadership positions will have to assimilate the equivalent of a college degree every seven years. And that will only let us keep up! Seventy-five percent of today's work force will require complete retraining by the turn of the century. A rapidly changing society has issued a challenge to promote lifelong learning. Progressive organizations will respond.

ORGANIZATION HABIT 2

Grow, Stabilize, Then Grow Some More

What do you think a graph showing the growth trend of an achieving company should look like? Should it be erratic, with low valleys and high peaks? Should it look like the side of a rolling hill, gradually but steadily moving upward? Or should it resemble a stairway—rising then plateauing, rising then plateauing?

American enterprise has paid a dear price for excessive growth. Most of the so-called high growth companies don't grow gradually. They climb like a jet fighter, and fall without a parachute. Companies that insist on a consistent growth rate in excess of 20 percent a year are destined to become troubled organizations fraught with debt, layoffs, and one crisis after another. Every few years, these companies trip themselves up, then realize they didn't leave adequate margin for error. These organizations don't walk to the edge and occasionally test it—they set up camp there.

The temptation to become a sprinter rather than a long distance runner is great, sometimes compulsive. There's something about flying without a parachute that makes flying more exciting . . . and more dangerous.

Do your business a favor. Grow, stabilize, then grow some more.

The darlings that make the headlines and receive the awards are the high-tech whiz kids. The entrepreneur who started a business in his college dorm is news—for awhile. But where is he in five or 10 years? Too often, the answer is bankrupt. The rock 'n rollers lack staying power. It's glamorous while it lasts, but it doesn't last long. High-tech and high growth are seductive.

So is the attraction to diversification. In reality, only a few individuals or organizations can effectively operate simultaneously in multiple industries. Developing a deep understanding of one product, service, or technology by continuously investing in knowledge is a better tactic. Get better and smarter at what you do, rather than trying to do everything.

Viable success stories formed over many years aren't the type of businesses journalists use much ink on. Yet these are the organizations led by people who understand business cycles go both ways. They understand the next significant event that happens to their organization might be negative. They know anyone can be a superstar for a while and that insistence on constant, rapid growth is foolhardy.

In the first paragraph of this Habit, I asked you to identify the best looking "growth graph" among three choices. My choice is the stair-step: organizations that grow, but also plateau to catch their breath, consolidate their knowledge, and fortify their finances. All the while they're planning and preparing for another step up a steeper part of the mountain.

Fill in the valleys and avoid the highest peaks. Grow, then stabilize. Then grow more and stabilize again.

ORGANIZATION HABIT 3

Partnerships Can Work if You Work at Them

If you told 100 successful entrepreneurs you were starting a business and asked them if you should seek a partner, at least 90 would give an immediate *no*. That advice is sound. It is usually better to go solo, but not always.

I have an equity partner of 20 years in one of my businesses and it pleases me to say our relationship has been excellent. Dean Neese and I were friends going in to the restaurant business. The good news is we're still friends.

Three years ago I was leaving by air charter for Des Moines to do a television commercial for our restaurant group. Dean and I also had an appointment with the local business magazine, which had asked for an interview the next time I was in town. While the pilot, producer, cameraman, and I were taking off—our instrument panel warned us our nose wheel had not fully retracted. After flying over the tower to let them take a look, they suggested we begin an emergency procedure to move the nose wheel manually. No luck. At the tower's request, we circled the airport for 10 minutes, our nose wheel stuck at 45 degrees. When the fire trucks were in position we made an emergency landing.

Our fears were correct. No nose wheel. We skidded to a safe stop and ran like hell for fear of fire. It turned out well, however. We jumped on another plane and maintained our schedule.

A couple of hours later, during our interview with the magazine, Dean told the reporter that she was talking to us on the day our business partnership came closest to dissolving because of my crash landing. That's not the way to become a sole proprietor. The experience made it clear there are worse things than partnerships.

One of the questions the reporter asked was, "How have you guys managed to remain not only partners, but friends, for more than 15 years?" Dean quipped "Distance." Indeed, our 280 mile separation has helped. But there are other ingredients, too.

Our partnership has flourished for many reasons, including:

1. *Distance, as referred to above.* We don't get in each other's way as often.

2. *Non-competing interests.* We're each responsible for different areas of the business, and while we do collaborate, Dean is location and operations oriented and I'm responsible for finance, administration, and planning. We seldom overlap.

3. *Consistent success.* We haven't had to deal with financial trauma, one of the foremost ways partnerships get into trouble.

4. *Separation of finances and management.* After almost 10 years of examining and researching franchising as a business concept, I acquired operating rights for a new Mexican fast food chain, Taco John's. I chose to operate the outlets in Des Moines, Iowa. Because I was 280 miles away in Sioux Falls, South Dakota, and for financial reasons, I invited Dean to be my partner. Dean had lived in the Des Moines area all his life and knew the city well.

   Importantly, I wasn't seeking management assistance from my partner. One of the most frequent reasons for partnership distress occurs when someone becomes a partner for both financial and management reasons. Seldom does the same person fill both of these needs effectively. Clear emphasis should be on one or the other.

5. *We share similar values.* We both have well-defined ethical boundaries. We treat each other, and our associates, honestly and fairly.

6. *Neither of us has ever been an employee of the company.* We've been able to avoid many of the conflicts created by salary disagreements, fringe packages, etc.

7. *Our plans are in writing.* The preparation of an annual strategic plan has been critical to the success of our partnership. We have agreed on our priorities and deadlines, know what we intend to accomplish, and who is responsible. Executing from a plan relieves potential partnership pain. And when disagreements do arise, the strategic plan often holds the key to effective and friendly resolution.

8. *We deal with futuristic needs proactively.* We are highly sensitive to discussing and resolving major issues before they hit crisis proportion. Fundamentally important areas like our cross-purchase agreement, funding in the case of disability or death, and succession planning are prime candidates for creating disagreement and are continually discussed.

Partnerships can and do work. There are occasions when bringing in a partner can add considerable value to the entrepreneurial effort. Be cautious, however. A partner must be secured for the right reasons, or you'll be sorry. And notice I've used *partner* in singular form only. Rarely will a partnership of more than two survive intact.

ORGANIZATION HABIT 4

Stay in Your Niche to Avoid the Ditch

"Never acquire a business you don't know how to run."

— *Robert W. Johnson*

Big is not as beautiful as it used to be.

One significant trend of the '90s will be the continuing emergence of the small, highly niched company whose business is to provide goods or services to a highly targeted audience.

For much of the 1980s, the dominate thinking was, "Big is better." We've learned that big not only isn't always better, sometimes it's worse. Bigness is increasingly more of a problem than a solution. The larger the company, the greater the tendency to move in illogical directions, to want to expand for no better reason than to grow. Many companies that haven't stuck to their knitting have paid heavy prices to learn they should have.

Ten years ago established companies were acquiring businesses by the bucketful. Many made acquisitions with little regard for what they knew about the industry they were entering. The worm has turned. Today, many of those acquisitions have become disappointments and smaller companies that know the industry are buying them back.

We have learned we can't be all things to all people. We've also learned we can achieve excellent results by staying in a business segment we understand.

The downsizing of American enterprise is an indicator of an increasingly entrepreneurial society. The small, highly niched and specialized business—with a tailored product serving a well-defined audience within a specific geographic area—is an important part of our future.

Creating a niche is like cutting a pie into 10 pieces instead of six. Breaking markets down into segments not previously targeted creates niches. It's a highly entrepreneurial process requiring early recognition of an opportunity.

There are other observable patterns that bode well for niche marketers.

Media Segmentation

The success of a niched business is highly dependent on its ability to offer products or services pertaining to a specific, identified audience. Accomplishing this requires reaching the intended, identified audience with a highly tailored and informational message.

Fortunately for the niched marketer, media is also becoming increasingly specialized. In the years ahead, there will be more opportunities to efficiently advertise and promote niched products to targeted audiences. The segmentation of America's media is, in itself, a confirmation of the increasing viability of a more thoroughly targeted marketplace. The total size of a medium's audience is becoming less meaningful, while the type of audience reached is becoming more meaningful.

The media wars of the future will be fought on the demographic and psychographic battleground. Mass media, such as daily newspapers and network television, will find themselves more and more out of step as viewers and advertisers make decisions more tightly aligned to their specific needs. Waste is out, targeted audiences are in.

Radio is becoming an increasingly important promotional vehicle. It's highly adaptable to audience segmentation and can readily change its target audience and its geographical coverage. Radio will increasingly anchor the promotional activities of businesses with a demographically targeted product or service.

Market Regionalization

Our economy's increasing segmentation will have other important impacts. For example, as target markets become narrower, there will be an increased need to reach further out geographically to find a market of adequate size. That introduces us to increased regionalization—another important futuristic influence. A narrower band of customers coming from a broader geographical area can be compared to the difference between a satellite sending a radio signal to a receiving dish on earth versus the broad distribution pattern of a standard AM or FM radio signal. They are both radio signals, but one has a more distant and specific target.

The news is good for business developers able to recognize a niched market opportunity. Niching is an important futuristic trend and offers terrific potential for alert entrepreneurial thinkers.

ORGANIZATION
HABIT 5

When Your Attorney Wins, Everyone Else Loses

"A society based on the letter of the law and never reaching any higher fails to take advantage of the full range of human possibilities. The letter of the law is too cold and formal to have a beneficial influence on society. Whenever the tissue of life is woven of legalistic relationships, it creates an atmosphere of spiritual mediocrity that paralyzes men's noblest impulses."

— Alexander Solzhenitsyn

My entrepreneurship has few absolute rules, but this is one of them: *If I wind up in court, as either plaintiff or defendant, I have failed.*

Here's an excerpt from a *Des Moines Register* column by Donald Kaul.

"Possibly you've heard the story about the fellow who opened a law office in a town that had no lawyers and found he wasn't making a living? Until a second lawyer started a practice across the street, that is. Then there was more than enough business for both of them. That is the nature of lawyers; the more of them there are, the merrier they get . . . the legal profession doesn't respond to the law of supply and demand. With lawyers, supply is demand."

If Donald Kaul's theory that lawyers create their own demand is right, we're in trouble. *Business Week* reported in its August 6, 1990, issue that we have 760,000 attorneys licensed to practice in the United States, and almost half have been admitted to the bar since 1980. Why such growth? Because, consistent with the American Way, it's a pretty good way to make a buck.

Why is law so lucrative? In part because lawyers make too many of our laws, and in part because business and consumers overuse legal services.

If America falls to its knees, I'm convinced it will be because our society stymied itself through excessive litigation. Our 760,000 attorneys serve 250 million people. By comparison, Japan has 110,000 lawyers for a population of 125 million. Japan has half our population yet gets along with only 15 percent of our attorneys. Putting it another way, we have more than three times as many lawyers per capita as Japan.

That isn't the only unfavorable comparison. The U.S. also has three times as many attorneys per capita as Great Britain, 30 times as many malpractice claims and 100 times as many product claims.

We have developed a mentality that causes us to want compensation for everything that goes wrong in our lives. We bring suit for the wildest reasons, and, of course, there is always a lawyer willing to help. We can complain all day about ambulance-chasing attorneys creating societal problems just to make a living. But until we take a fundamentally different view of our legal system we're dead in the water.

Business, as one of the major consumers of legal services, needs to set the example in making our society less legalistic. Finding ways to use fewer legal services is the only way to set that example.

We have become too willing to hire a lawyer to do what we don't need a lawyer for. Communication is at the top of the list. When we have a disagreement with someone, our initial response is to hire a lawyer to talk to the other party. Why not do the

---

talking ourselves? Did the attorney go to communication school
. . . or to law school?

Our business sector spends millions upon millions of unnecessary dollars annually for legal services that are really communication services we should do for ourselves. Don't hire a mouthpiece. Have the courage to talk to the disagreeing party yourself. Approach the problem straight on, saving money, anxiety, and time.

Like business people, some lawyers are good, some not so good. Many have acceptable ethical standards, others don't. Legal profession ethics are no better or no worse than other cross sections of society. Some lawyers, however, do our society harm by seeking remuneration for actions not worthy of the effort. In the process, they hold institutions and individuals accountable for unrealistic performance standards.

Legal scholar Walter Olson, in his book *The Litigation Explosion: What Happened When America Unleashed the Lawsuit*, discusses at length the abuse of the legal system and how it is dragging our economy down. Although plaintiff lawyers may not agree with him, most citizens do. Simply put, we're going to court to right every possible wrong—except, of course, the wrong done to defendants hauled into court for frivolous reasons.

We can fix our legal cancer by following Canada in abolishing the contingency fee and making the losing courtroom opponent pay the fees of the winning side.

America suffers from a self-inflicted wound. We have too many attorneys. And the more work we give them, the more we're going to have. Do your leadership and our society a favor. Look aggressively for alternatives before calling a lawyer. Communicate . . . negotiate . . . but don't litigate.

Remember, when your attorney wins, everyone else loses.

ORGANIZATION HABIT 6

To Over-Consult Is an Insult

"Consultant: an ordinary guy more than 50 miles from home."

— *Eric Sevareid*

There are an estimated 50,000 business consultants in the U.S., and I'm one of them. Most of us aren't any good.

Business consultants charge a fee to try to do for others what most of them can't do for themselves. It has been said they are clever people who borrow your watch to give you the time, then charge you for the information. Highly entrepreneurial folks.

Many consultants make a living well beyond the benefits of the services provided. Otherwise sophisticated business people frequently hire consultants who have little expertise and even less personal business experience.

Consultants and attorneys have many similarities. There are too many, business relies on them too heavily, and they are often more obstacle-oriented than opportunity-oriented. Unlike attorneys, however, consultants can hang out their shingles anywhere, anytime—thus assuring the consumer a broad variation of skills and competence. I've seen many who don't have a clue about what they're doing.

If you have genuine need for a good consultant, be particular. Here are some suggestions:

1. Know as precisely as possible what your problem is and match the consultant to it. Check at least three references he or she has helped with similar problems.

2. Interview three to five consultants before deciding on one. You may wish to include a CPA firm with a consulting division if they are experienced in your area of need.

3. After making your selection, require a written agreement describing the scope of the project, timing and amount of compensation, type of written report to be issued, and completion date.

ORGANIZATION HABIT 7

It's Time to Become a Working Environmentalist

If you're the boss, take care of the environment—your working environment. You are in charge of the company's air quality, noise pollution, and climate. This is your opportunity to determine the environmental conditions you and your associates work in.

There's a sales rep who calls on me regularly, and every time he's in my office he tells me what a nice office we have and how professional we are. He has also shared that if I were to visit his office he would take me in through the back door because the front lobby is so disgusting. If that weren't enough, he tells of his CEO walking up and down the halls without shoes, surely not a habit to emulate.

Working environments, as shown in the above example, have a significant impact on visitors. Of equal importance, however, is the impact it has on your fellow workers.

I know my co-workers appreciate having a pleasant place to work. They tell me so. And I also encourage them to tell me when there's a deficiency that needs attention, which they do.

Being a "workplace environmentalist" isn't a matter of responsibility. It's a matter of productivity, worker attitudes, customer image, and employee retention. So don't do it just because you're a sweetheart. Do it because it's good for business. And it is!

ORGANIZATION HABIT 8

Every Organization Has a Culture and Is Therefore Eligible for Culture Shock

In the early 1980s I served on the board of directors of a Los Angeles company that did business in several countries. We came upon shaky times, encouraged our CEO to leave and went about the business of replacing him. We enjoyed a strong national reputation and had several excellent candidates. We selected what we thought was an extraordinary individual to become our new CEO.

It didn't work. In less than six months he was gone, replaced by a long-time vice president with more friends in the organization but fewer of the needed skills.

The CEO we hired from the outside was very good. His credentials were strong coming in and were proven in the short time he was there. So why didn't he succeed? Competence doesn't always win the day. He created systems and provided solutions that were appropriate. In doing so, however, he insulted tradition and shocked the company's culture. It wasn't the type of cultural experience the company needed.

With the benefit of hindsight, his style wasn't in step with the 50-year tradition of the company. He was the first outsider the organization ever had in a top job. He challenged the good-old-boy network—and the good old boys won!

Businesses are mini-societies with their own culture. As with individuals, rapid-fire cultural changes create havoc. Newly appointed leaders need to learn about the organization's heritage and accommodate it during the transitional period.

Leading is a cultural experience. Be sure not to give it a shock.

ORGANIZATION
HABIT 9

Keeping Your Organization I/U Balanced

The I stands for Innovation, the U for Utility. Let's simplify this by breaking all organizations into two types: entrepreneurial and non-entrepreneurial.

In an entrepreneurial environment an organization is prone toward innovation. Their experimental attitude is a big plus unless taken to excess.

When excessively involved in pursuing innovation, the organization becomes mired in tinkering and adjusting. Innovation becomes the end in itself. The organization gets so involved in making changes that making a living receives little attention. This organization tinkers itself into mediocrity, perhaps extinction.

The other type of organization in our hypothetical example is non-entrepreneurial. It exists in stark contrast to the entrepreneurial enterprise, paying little attention to anything resembling innovation. Growth is minimal; it's a dull place to work. Things are done the way they were twenty years ago. This utilitarian organization is archaic and its performance shows it.

Neither of our hypothetical examples are achieving organizations. Both are out of balance, although in opposite directions.

Excellent organizations have an equilibrium, a corporate gyroscope that keeps their innovative flair and utilitarian need for profit in balance. Each supports the other interdependently. A company that's balanced effectively blends the virtues of innovation with the utility of making a living.

―――――――――――――――――――――――――――

ORGANIZATION HABIT 10

Internal Informality— External Formality

Defining the organization's personality, its degree of formality, is a key decision for the entrepreneurial executive. Would you describe the personality of your organization as formal, informal, or both?

Ninety-five percent of the companies I have seen are single-personality companies. That is, they are either formal or informal, but not both.

The other five percent possess a dual personality—at times formal, at times informal. This is my kind of organization.

Successful entrepreneurial organizations are internally informal. That doesn't mean nobody wears a tie to work. It means people feel comfortable talking with each other in a highly verbal environment. It means they write fewer internal memos, favoring more direct, eyeball-to-eyeball communication. Internal informality fosters a productive working environment. People feel better and express themselves more freely. This higher level of unstructured internal communication also pays dividends by delighting the customer. Why? Because the employee is more accustomed to verbal give and take.

The flip side of the dual organizational personality is external formality. Ever notice how some organizations have a tendency toward misunderstandings with suppliers and customers? Misunderstandings are a business disease that afflict the externally informal.

The difference between mediocrity and excellence is often not much more than a matter of detail. Externally informal organizations operate with a handshake, not a contract. They don't deal in detail. They agree to something on the telephone but don't follow up the conversation with the important "Here's what I understand" letter or memo to file. They deal in a world of wandering approximates, rather than specific understandings. They regularly miss deadlines and goals.

External informality isn't accidental. I believe it's caused by laziness. And by managers who aren't comfortable writing a good letter. Given a choice, they would rather say it than write it. Too bad. Agreements and understandings need to be recorded.

Achievement requires an ability to communicate not as you wish, but as the situation demands. Competent organizational leaders know when to say it informally and when to write it formally.

Internal informality and external formality are trademarks of winning organizations. Keep it loose on the inside and tight on the outside.

VII

ACHIEVING THROUGH LEADERSHIP

"Our chief want in life is somebody who will make us do what we can."

— *Ralph Waldo Emerson*

Have you ever heard Winston Churchill, Franklin D. Roosevelt, or John Kennedy referred to as a manager? Certainly not. They were leaders.

Even our top universities have yet to offer a degree in leadership. I doubt they ever will. Leadership is, to a large extent, learned on the firing line. I have yet to meet a student fresh from campus who is a leader. Maybe a manager. Maybe a potential leader. But not a leader.

Reading this chapter won't create a leader, either. However, its 15 Leadership Habits will help you sort through the difference between managing and leading and offer road markers to guide you on your journey to ever-improving leadership techniques.

LEADERSHIP
HABIT 1

Tantalizing Tips for Pursuing Leadership Excellence

"Good is not good where better is expected."
— *Thomas Fuller*

There are dozens of good books on excellence, but not all are readily applicable to leading the small- or medium-sized business. The following keys to excellence will be of particular benefit to the leader looking for a brief, high-impact reference.

1. *Constantly put yourself in the employee's shoes.* Look at your decisions from their perspective. Your intentions may be good, but perceptions are what count. Do a constant perception check.

2. *Communicate your vision.* Give your teammates the opportunity to buy in to your goals. Make your vision their vision. Break down your vision into small increments. Reward each incremental achievement.

3. *Make sure everyone on staff has a reason to feel important.* The quickest way to accomplish this is to be sure you don't have too many people. Within a working environment that has a sense of urgency, a need for everyone to carry weight creates the opportunity for self-importance. More people cause more problems, not the least of which is an awareness

by employees that not everyone getting a paycheck is necessary. Paranoia sets in, energy level goes south.

Limit participants. Keep the organization trim to create a better working environment. Rather than ride the ego trip of adding people to support your growth, work with current staff to find ways to increase productivity. When individual productivity increases, find a way for it to benefit everyone—not only increased profits for the owner, but better pay and increased job security for productive employees.

4. *Take a chance on gifted people.* Sometimes they are a delight, sometimes difficult. But you can't achieve prominence or create substantial wealth without surrounding yourself with talent. Find a way to let winners win.

5. *Establish regular, consistent opportunities to communicate.* Bring in a pizza for lunch, show videotapes on relevant topics, or make departments responsible for staff meetings on a rotating basis. Be creative. Keep everyone feeling good about their work and their future.

6. *Celebrate events and accomplishments unexpectedly.* Rigidity is out. Flexibility is in. Find ways to change the pace, to create excitement. Offer an extra afternoon off on a beautiful summer day. Do the unexpected. The more people expect something, the less they appreciate it and vice versa.

7. *Put employees at risk.* I don't mean on the edge of their seat waiting to see if they are about to lose their jobs. Simply be sure they know what they do is necessary work and that you are counting on them. Add importance to their daily duties. Give them a feeling of ownership in positive results.

8. *Develop outstanding incentive compensation opportunities.* This is a great way to convey a sense of ownership. Make everyone a bean counter. Give them a vested interest in providing customer delight, as well as prudent management of expenses and growth.

9. *Treat each employee like your best customer.* The hard reality is we can't expect an employee to care for customers unless the employee feels cared for by the employer. Unhappy employees create unhappy customers. Delighted employees create delighted customers. The choice is yours.

LEADERSHIP HABIT 2

To Lead or to Manage—
A Million Dollar Question

We manage ourselves and lead others.

We manage things and lead people.

Management is a discipline. Leadership is an art.

Managers bring order to complexity. Leaders create visions and strategies.

Managers are practical. Leaders are conceptual.

Managers react to market trends. Leaders anticipate them.

Managers play lead trumpet. Leaders conduct the orchestra.

Managers implement institutional values. Leaders create them.

Managers are sometimes loud. Leaders are often quiet.

Managers execute a plan. Leaders write it.

Managers do things right. Leaders do the right thing.

Managers analyze. Leaders conceptualize.

Managers administer. Leaders inspire.

Managers accomplish goals. Leaders influence behavior.

Managers do. Leaders design.

Unselfishness is a special distinguishing characteristic of leadership. There is no such thing as a selfish leader.

Leaders give.

Bill Byrne

LEADERSHIP HABIT 3

You Can Tell Leaders Anything, But They May Not Agree

My vote for Entrepreneur of the 1980s goes to Ted Turner. Since 1980, he has developed Cable News Network into what many describe as the world's most important news organization. The impact of CNN was felt with the fall of communism in the Eastern Bloc and during the Persian Gulf War. Clearly, the world is different because of CNN.

When Turner announced the formation of CNN, he was universally ridiculed as a dreamer. Later asked during a BBC interview how he knew a market existed for 24-hour television news, Turner replied, "I just knew it."

Turner's decision was courageous. It wasn't based on massive market research. His decision was, to a large extent, based on intuition. That's how it is with many significant accomplishments. The courageous leader has a sixth sense, believes he or she understands something others don't, and sets out to prove it. More often than not, a strong intuitive idea hatched by an entrepreneurial mind is a winner.

Indeed, decision making is more a process of filtered intuition than of numbers, graphs, and research. That's one reason why new ventures have trouble raising money. Only one person has the vision, and it's hard to communicate one's intuition.

Through experience, seasoned decision makers come to understand the best opinion is their own. No amount of advice can replace a strong instinct. That doesn't mean the opportunity always works. It means one's intuitive track record is a significant decision input. It means the ability to think contrarily is important. And it means the *consensus view* is just as often wrong as right. Experts are a dime a dozen. The achiever pays little attention to their often errant consensus.

Many significant achievements find little support during the initial stages of consideration. If you thoughtfully and intuitively believe in an opportunity, stay with it. Even though others may disagree.

LEADERSHIP HABIT 4

Vince Lombardi Was Wrong. Winning Isn't the Only Thing.

Whether you win or lose may depend on the quality of the competition you select.

For years I have played in a regular golf foursome. My playing partners—Don, Keel, and Ray have each won at least one state golf championship, far surpassing my credentials. On a typical day, I take the most strokes getting around the course.

Am I a loser? My preference is to think I'm not. I believe I benefit from being able to play with better golfers. There are plenty of golf games I can put together to assure myself the lowest score in the group. Would that make me a winner?

Some determine who won and who lost by looking at the score card. Others look at the quality of the competition. Still others define winning internally—if you did your best, you're a winner.

Losing isn't always bad. It depends on how you define it.

LEADERSHIP
HABIT 5

He Who Talks First Loses

Public speakers and negotiators have a similar need—both should be comfortable with periods of silence. The speaker increases impact with a brief pause, while the negotiator shuts up to see if the other party will commit first. When negotiating, he who talks first loses.

Why do we negotiate? Because we want something we can't get without someone else's agreement. Although we sometimes feel like we want to say "take it or leave it," we play the negotiating game, hoping to more amicably fulfill our need.

We often negotiate with people with whom we will develop an ongoing business relationship. That amplifies the negatives of trying to back someone into a corner, forcing them to come out with egg on their face.

Theoretically, everything is negotiable—price, warranty, interest rate, transaction fees, payment terms, etc. An effective negotiator begins with a prioritized need list and never loses sight of those priorities. He knows going in he won't get everything he wants, so setting priorities is important.

We frequently picture negotiation as two or more people with gritted teeth, locked in a room, staring across a table with bloodshot eyes. That's pure fantasy. Successful negotiations are conducted in a non-adversary, non-hostile environment. Effective negotiation isn't just taking. It's giving and taking. There's no need to negotiate with someone who will give you everything you want, so don't plan on coming away with it 100 percent your way.

By definition, effective negotiation is a process that lets both parties get what's most important to them. The desired outcome of a negotiation is when each can honestly say, "I got what was most important to me, and I think the other folks did, too." Both parties need to call it a win, and unless each has the same top priority, it's possible both will succeed.

Here are some rules for effective negotiation:

1. *He who talks first loses.* The emphasis is on listening, waiting for the other party to commit first.

2. *Always know your priorities.* You will have to give. Know going in where you will, and where you don't want to.

3. *Be deliberate but not unbending.* There is a time to win and a time to let go.

4. *Find a way for all parties to win.* There should be something good in the outcome for everyone.

5. *Agree on an agenda.* Like all business meetings, participants will benefit from agreeing to a general format before beginning discussions.

6. *Offer ideas for settlement.* Remain true to your priorities but don't be afraid to keep options open that are acceptable to you.

7. *Always be decent.* The cost of a negotiation turning ugly can be high. A lawsuit, or having the other party walk away from an opportunity you really wanted, can be expensive. Settle it if you possibly can. Avoid going home without an agreement.

9. *By all means, put the agreement in writing.* No need to be legalistic. Just a straightforward memo, properly signed and dated, is adequate.

Negotiating is an art worthy of frequent use. As discussed in the last chapter, we too often move to the courtroom to settle disputes people could solve by talking it out. Anything we can do to enhance the role of negotiating in our litigious society creates a winning opportunity for everyone.

Bill Byrne

LEADERSHIP HABIT 6

The Power of Punctuality

Punctuality is a habit. So is tardiness. I would bet good money that habitual lifestyle, not uncontrollable circumstances, cause more than 90 percent of the instances of tardiness.

Habitually tardy people have little idea of its cost. One person late for a meeting held among five people stymies the productivity of all five. Tardiness is one of our biggest productivity robbers.

Research has shown up to 96 percent of dissatisfied customers don't complain—but 90 percent of them silently go elsewhere. The same is true of tardiness. People don't complain much about it, but they nonetheless have strong feelings.

I'll bet you know someone who plays the late game for effect. He or she is too important or too busy to be on time. There are just not enough hours in the day. In reality, there are plenty of hours in the day. Tardiness is an attempt to overcome an inferiority complex. A *grand entrance* supposedly increases one's sense of self-importance. But then why did someone say, "The early bird gets the worm?"

At the very heart and soul of our professional existence lies our ability to meet the expectations of others. We make commitments and we make promises. If we wish to be effective, and to be perceived as such, we have to meet expectations. And that starts with maintaining ritualistic punctuality.

LEADERSHIP
HABIT 7

Tell Me, Are You Thinking, or Are You Feeling

When I discovered the difference between thinking and feeling, it revolutionized my life. Thinking is a thought. Feeling is an emotion. Knowing whether the person you're communicating with is thinking or feeling makes all the difference in the world to your communicating success.

A match between someone feeling an emotion against another thinking a thought disables communication. When at least one of the parties recognizes whether the other is thinking thoughts or feeling emotions, they can connect. Both parties must then get on the same frequency to communicate effectively.

The left brain thinker and the right brain feeler often find themselves at odds because of this basic difference in communication style. Each style has its benefits and weaknesses, depending on the topic. If you've ever tried to make a thinker out of a feeler, or vice versa, you're aware that it's difficult, if not impossible. However, there is a way to bridge the gap.

The first step is to pause and notice whether the other party is feeling or thinking. Often they'll tell you! They may say, "I *think* this and so" or "I *feel* . . . " Quietly understand where they are coming from, then move in their direction and make connection. Become rational and thoughtful or feeling and emotional, depending on the situation.

The communicator who understands the difference between thinking and feeling and is aware of it during a transaction is a comfortable step ahead in any discussion.

LEADERSHIP HABIT 8

It's OK to be Tough as Long as You're Fair

If I were to list the Bill Byrne "Rules Of Supervision," the first one would be the title of this Habit.

There is always a job to be done, and you have every right to expect that it gets done. Employees want leaders who provide guidelines and standards that delineate expectations. They also prefer a leader they know they can count on in difficult situations. Someone who is decent, dependable, and fair.

I asked an executive secretary how she liked working for her boss. Her answer was surprising. "I love it," she responded. "I have to work hard, but I always know what he expects. His consistency is important to me." Indeed, one of the primary requirements of effective supervision is clarifying the agenda, "grabbing order out of chaos."

Ask for a hard day's work. Good people don't mind. Many prefer it. But do it fairly. Ask the same from everyone. No politics, no favorites. Clear the non-performers out to make room for achievers to grow deeper roots.

At times, toughness is a required characteristic. People are attracted to organizations lead by individuals seen as competent and caring, individuals who know where they are going. People respect leaders who possess fair-minded toughness. Toughness is tolerable when fairness is its partner.

LEADERSHIP HABIT 9

Don't Over Commit-tee

"A decision is what a man makes when he can't find anybody to serve on a committee."
— *Fletcher Knebel*

There are times when leaders can choose not to lead. It's alright to say no.

Involvement in community affairs is necessary to being a complete individual. We all want to give something back. When the format for community participation is committees and boards, true leaders choose from two alternatives. They get involved when there is a passion for the cause and say no when the passion doesn't exist.

Community organizations need more than committee members—they need good ones. Too many want to join, too few want to work. If your heart isn't in it, your contribution will show it. How about declining the invitation and giving the chair to someone who genuinely cares about community service, someone who will really participate?

Decision quality and frequency is inversely proportional to the number of people involved. When it comes to competent decision-making, more is not merrier. Know yourself and your patience level before accepting a committee or board invitation. If you say yes, pull your weight. Make as much of a difference as possible within the constraints of group management. If, on the other hand, it's not in your heart, do yourself and the organization a favor. Don't join just for appearances.

LEADERSHIP
HABIT 10

When Personal and Positional Leadership Come in the Same Body, You Have a Winner

Does leadership strength come from one's persona, position, or both?

Community leadership status is as often awarded on the basis of position as for personal leadership ability. Positional leadership occurs when a bank board, the United Way board, or the board of directors of the Chamber of Commerce quickly invites the new manager of the local utility, hospital, major department store, or other significant business—who just came to town—to join their board. The casual observer wonders what credentials this person has to become so rapidly integrated into community decision making. Sometimes, the individual is of such personal reputation and ability the choice is obvious. At other times, the only credential is *position*.

Personal and positional leadership can be as different as night and day. One perk many corporate managers especially enjoy is the ability to become a BMIT (big man in town) through employer affiliation. Positional leadership is a shortcut to community leadership. But it doesn't hold a candle to the power of personal leadership.

Personal leadership comes from within. That's where the action is. When savvy community organizations want to add talent to their board or committees they find the personal leaders. These individuals generate their power independent of position and transcend the need to ride organizational coattails.

Personal leadership always outlasts positional leadership. If your interest is attracting talent, not status, go for personal leaders. If they come with titles, so much the better.

LEADERSHIP HABIT 11

Will You Listen to Me?

Pause a minute. Think of three people you know who qualify as honest-to-goodness leaders. Now consider two or three characteristics you believe common to all three. What characteristic first comes to mind? Their charisma? Their good looks? Their sense of humor? Probably not. More likely, they are apt to be thought of as informed *inhalers of information.* They are inquisitive and have a genuine interest in you and your subject matter. They are more inclined to listen than to talk and are likely to control the agenda, sculpting inquiries targeted to elicit specific knowledge.

If you consider yourself a leader, chances are excellent you are also a good listener, with the following listening characteristics:

... listening more than half the time

... constantly asking questions, using the answers as an opportunity to assimilate knowledge

... listening on a non-discriminatory basis by giving equal attention to men and women, young and old, rich and poor

... having good eye contact with the speaker

... giving visual feedback—affirming what is said by shaking your head, voicing agreement, etc.

... clarify what was said, if in doubt

... not interrupting except to learn more

Listening doesn't come naturally. Sometimes it's a joy, sometimes work. Regardless, everyone deserves an equal opportunity to have your ear. Knowledge comes from the most unexpected sources.

LEADERSHIP HABIT 12

Leadership in Balance Is Leadership at Its Best

Success can be superficial, but not when it's in balance. Balanced success includes not only one's *financial self* but the *spiritual self* as well. Balanced leaders live a multifaceted, enriched life full of personal satisfaction. They know their *real self* and never abandon the core values which impact their decisions and judgments.

Everyone has what I call an "essential self," the real us that lives in our heart. If we are true to our *essential self*, we balance the needs of spouse, family, money, and profession. The needs of the day don't sweep us away. Our perspective is long-term, not whimsical. We do things for the right reasons.

Balance provides the strength to endure painful times, whether personal or professional. It gives us an ethical vantage point from which to watch the effects of a particular course of action. Balanced leaders are harmoniously focused on what is permanent, differentiating it from what is just passing by. The balanced leader's *essential self* acts as a personal center of gravity that withstands the turbulence entrepreneurial leaders face. It coordinates what we believe with how we behave and constantly works to reconcile the difference between the two.

Our world is a winding, sometimes dangerous road with many unplanned potholes, corners, and intersections. If we are to complete our journey content that we have served well, we need to live a balanced life. To have all the money in the world and lose your family is not success. To know all the powerful people in the world and not have friends is not success; and to be known by everyone and loved by no one is not success. Our *essential self* knows when it's betrayed by appearances and the false gods of power and possessions.

Clinging to a balanced *essential self* provides two lifetime guarantees: That success will be defined by the right perspective and over the long-term. Balanced success is dependent on a rigid set of beliefs which call for constant attention as we move through the alternatives of personal and professional life.

> A 67-year-old executive was dying of cancer. He lived a good life, became a multimillionaire and raised four kids in a happy home. Asked by a friend how he would live life differently if given another chance, he replied, "I would have spent my money sooner." That is an insightful response for those who have yet to understand we can't take it with us.

A familiar television ad asks "How do you spell relief?" Observers of achieving leaders ask "How do you spell success?" One way to spell it is B-A-L-A-N-C-E.

LEADERSHIP HABIT 13

If It's Lonely at the Top, You Should Have Taken the Stairs

"There is always room at the top, but there's no time to sit down."

— *Helen Downey*

You have everything you could ever want. And you're not a happy person? It happens a lot. Life at the top isn't always what it's bragged up to be.

Reaching "the top" too easily can be more unfulfilling than waging a lifelong struggle to make ends meet. Grinding out the steps on each rung of life's ladder brings fulfillment and self-esteem. There's nothing better than feeling good about what you have because you earned it.

Years ago I had a friend who made a respectable living specializing in a narrow business segment. He and his wife had two preschool kids and ostensibly had a good family life. When a competitor wanted to enter his specialty segment, they approached him and offered a huge compensation package if he would jump ship and run their new division. He made the move.

For the next few years he achieved only mediocre results. One of the contributing factors, I believe, was that he didn't feel he deserved the financial windfall. His lifestyle changed. He began drinking heavily. His wife moved out for a short while. His mood became sullen.

From the outside looking in, he was one lucky dude. From the inside looking out, he was in hell on earth.

Perhaps he attributed his sudden pile of money to luck, believing he didn't deserve it. Perhaps he drank so others would blame drinking instead of lack of ability for not achieving the results his new employer expected. Or perhaps his changed behavior was a result of how undeserving he felt. One thing is for sure—the money didn't bring him self-esteem. If you don't feel you deserve it, you won't feel good about having it.

Life at the top runs the emotional gamut from loneliness to happiness. Those of us who have to climb the stairs of achievement may not be so bad off after all. When we get there, our chances of enjoying it are much better.

LEADERSHIP
HABIT 14

Sometimes Leading Means Following

In 1985, my wife and I were invited to a cocktail party to view promotional scenes of a would-be movie. More than half of the footage was to be shot in the Black Hills of South Dakota. It was the first time in more than 30 years a major portion of a movie had been filmed there.

The producer was a South Dakota native living in Los Angeles. She met her husband, also the movie's screenwriter and director, in film school. They had one very low-budget movie under their belts and wanted to try another on a larger scale. They came home to finance it.

I met Barbara Schock and husband, Rex Pickett, at the cocktail party. After hearing their presentation and looking at their film clips, I became enamored by their film-making talent and, more importantly, their tremendous sense of commitment to their film project. When they called the next day, we set up an appointment to discuss the marketing questions dominating their minds.

During our visit I provided suggestions on how they could effectively market their limited partnership and also offered to invest a small amount. Besides relatives, I was their first investor. My investment was more focused on supporting their gutsy entrepreneurship than on a high return.

Barbara and Rex, as much as any entrepreneurs I had met, deserved a chance to make their dream come true. I wanted to help. After considerable discussion, I agreed to become their executive producer, a title given the person in charge of the production's business side. By this time I had invested a little more money and considerably more time.

My executive producer contract was for one dollar and the opportunity to have an impact on the movie and learn a new kind of entrepreneurship. Although the movie's budget was in place before I became involved, the three of us felt my primary value would be bean counting and marketing the movie to a distributor when completed.

Rex Pickett had written what I thought was a great screenplay, counterpointing drama and humor. They raised the money. It was time to transplant the screenplay to film. The journey was long and challenging. We finally finished filming, after many detours caused by weather and budget overruns. Considering the circumstances, getting it completed was quite an achievement.

The confluence of many circumstances removed me from much of the direct marketing involvement I had contemplated when the project began. It wasn't my movie, so I went with the flow. I stood on the sidelines waiting to be called into the game. Except for a couple of plays, I wasn't. The movie was marketed, ineffectively in my opinion. I stood by and watched it happen, uncomfortable with the process and aware of the probable result.

I made a choice. I remained true to the philosophy that attracted me to the project in the first place. I tried to help two entrepreneurs who had deep commitment and substantial talent. Though naive in many aspects of the business, Rex and Barbara deserved a chance to prove they could do it. That was why I jumped on board and why I stayed there. For the first time in my entrepreneurial life I felt an unempowered need to follow, to let two new entrepreneurs learn for themselves.

This experience wasn't a financial success for me or the many other helpful investors. But there are times to give something back. This was one of mine. I learned much and met many terrific people. I was there to see the movie was completed against heavy odds.

From Hollywood to Deadwood played in theaters throughout the country and is available on video worldwide. I'm proud of it.

LEADERSHIP HABIT 15

How Do Leaders Create Wealth from Mistakes?

"Good judgement comes from experience. And where does experience come from? Experience comes from bad judgement."

— *Mark Twain*

The answer to the question posed in the title of this Habit is that mistakes create knowledge, which in turn helps assure the alert leader he or she won't make the same mistake again.

In business, the more mistakes you make the more likely you will achieve greatness, provided one big mistake doesn't take you down—and provided you make the same mistake only once. Mistakes are inherently important to achievers. Seldom can one start from scratch and accumulate significant wealth without periods of riding a roller coaster.

Leadership is an art. It defies scientific formula or arithmetic calculation. Leadership is touch, feel, instinct, and thought. It's learning, failing, and growing.

My entrepreneurial leadership has been far from perfect. I've made many mistakes. Some really hurt. The good news is I haven't made one big enough to take me for a tumble. And all have helped me become better at what I do and more appreciative of success when it arrives. Here are the Bill Byrne "Top Ten Mistakes Made by Leaders of New Businesses":

1. *Improper pricing.* Inexperienced business owners get jittery when setting prices. The overwhelming tendency is to go into business with prices that are too low and don't allow adequate profit margins. If the business survives, slim margins often lock the organization into underachievement.

   Why not go into business with unrealistically low prices, attract customers, then raise prices to where they should be? Because it usually doesn't work. The customer feels cheated, which jeopardizes loyalty. Pay keen attention to pricing, especially before opening the business.

2. *Numerical ignorance.* Is there a numbers person in your business? If not, get one. You don't need a CPA, but someone in the organization must understand its numbers. You can't create significant wealth in an environment of numerical ignorance—or what I call "numnorance."

3. *Poor timing.* Timing is almost everything. If the timing of an idea is not perfect, it is better for owners with limited capital to be a little late rather than a little early. Breaking new ground is slow, expensive work.

4. *Competing with someone who is too dominant.* Unless it's a new industry, be cautious if a single competitor has more than 30 percent of the market. Dominant competition is traditionally well-capitalized, patient, even ruthless. They play for keeps.

5. *You left your niche.* Remember what you went into business to do, and be as patient as possible. Diluting your original plan with extraneous, unfocused activities is dangerous. Advantageous diversification is accomplished from a position of strength. It's fine to be open to new ideas, but don't engage in random wandering.

   The prime opportunities of the next 10 years will be in well-defined, targeted niches. Stay close to a specific audience. Broaden only if you have planned the move thoroughly and if it fits your strategic niche.

6. *Lack of control over suppliers.* If you are buying components, for example, and assembling or altering them to make

a finished product, you should be sure there are multiple sources of supply. If you don't, you could wind up between a supplier and a banker.

7. *Not differentiating between cash and profit.* In the first five years of a business, cash flow management is more important than profit. In spite of this, most pay more attention to profit. Believe it or not, profit may not keep you in business. Cash will.

8. *Excess pursuit.* Growing fast is not all it's bragged up to be. Growth requires talent and cash. If you don't have a good amount of each, better watch out. Grow within your means.

9. *Setting customer expectations you don't live up to.* Promising more than you deliver causes trouble for any business. For a new business, it is almost sure death.

10. *Talent deficiency.* I saved the most important until last. Find talent. Reward talent. Respect talent. Keep talent. Significant achievement escapes those who don't attract and keep talent.

VIII

FOCUSING ON YOUR FUTURE

"We can do only what we think we can do. We can be only what we think we can be. We can have only what we think we can have. What we do, what we are, what we have all depend upon what we think."
— *Robert Collier*

Most of us spend a lifetime answering the ultimate question—what do we want to be when we grow up? Thankfully, it's never fully answered. If it were, our achievement would come to an end. So we continue to ask. Somewhere in the contemplation of the answer is the essence of what we will become.

Our priorities for the future—what we want to be—are constantly changing. The Habits in this chapter point us in the direction of a more fulfilling, ethical, and rewarding future.

FUTURISTIC HABIT 1

Make Yourself a Healthy Commitment

We can help ourselves and those in our professional environment obtain a lasting gift, the gift of health. When we practice, encourage, and reinforce healthful lifestyles we are leading in a most productive way. Good health and high productivity go hand in hand. Healthy people are more productive and so is their organization.

Smoking, excessive consumption of alcohol, and couch potato behavior not only reduce individual and organizational productivity, but the enjoyment of life as well. What can we do to enhance the healthful future for ourselves, our associates, and our organization?

First, consider drastic action. When an office introduces smoking bans or drug testing programs for example, most workers appreciate them. They understand the value of health-sensitive programs and are receptive. Be bold.

Second, guide your actions by the desires and rights of those most sensitive to good health. It is legal to discriminate against smokers. Point your leadership concern toward the healthful needs of the nonsmoker rather than the selfish desires of the smoker. Don't hire smokers if you or your associates want a smokeless environment. You and others in your workplace have a right to clean air. And, I would propose, effective leadership requires that you provide it.

Third, be sensitive to employee stress levels. Is your leadership style a *stress inducer* or a *stress reducer*? Step back and check your leadership behavior. Are you predictable or unpredictable? Much of the stress in our working environment is unnecessary, caused by superiors who respond emotionally and unpredictably. Too many so-called leaders are guilty of foisting unpleasant surprises on employees, causing the worker to worry about what will happen next. Lack of predictability creates stress; predictability reduces it. You may be inflicting unhealthy stress in your workplace and not know it.

Be predictable. Demonstrate to your people that you are not likely to throw negative surprises at them. Create a trusting work environment. It will reduce stress levels while increasing healthfulness and productivity.

The best way for us to encourage a healthful workplace is to lead by example. If we as leaders live healthfully, odds increase that our followers will also. Winning habits become contagious over time. The health payoff is huge for both the individual and the organization.

I was 35 before I recognized the benefits of, and need for, a healthful lifestyle. The following magazine column, written in March, 1990, tells my personal story.

I just celebrated an important anniversary.

It was a Wednesday, about 7:00 in the evening. Son Jason and I were headed home with sandwiches for the family.

It was the tail end of a thirteen hour business day with little rest and too much caffeine.

The sandwiches didn't make it home. And neither did we.

Instead, we drove to a nearby emergency room. I thought I was having a heart attack.

Jason and I were there only about a half hour before we found out that no, it wasn't a heart attack. But the hospital staff was puzzled, and for the next two days I was hooked up to everything in sight as they tried to solve the mystery.

My problem? It turned out to be high blood pressure. The solution? Backing off my schedule, eliminating caffeine, taking some high blood pressure pills, and starting an exercise program.

Looking back, the experience was full of lessons. I learned that bodies need more tender love and care when they reach 35. The greater lesson, however, was the value of exercise.

My life changed 10 years ago. It was in February, 1980, that Dick Friess, a Sioux Falls doctor somewhat ahead of his time, told me I should take responsibility for my own wellness, and a good part of that meant establishing a regular exercise program.

I took his words seriously. All he suggested was that I take my heart rate up to about 140 beats a minute for 10-12 minutes four times a week. My wife Lynne now exercises too, and we're on our third bedroom exercycle. The 10-12 minute workouts are now 20 to 30 and include not only biking but occasional floor aerobics and jogging for variety.

I feel great, have more stamina and weigh three pounds more than when I graduated from college. Essentially, what I did to improve my health was set aside some time most every day for myself to exercise. It was an important change in my life. I grabbed the bull by the horns and wrestled it to the ground. And if I can do it so can you.

It's not too late to make a serious resolution for the '90s. Talk to your doctor and get with the program. Set some exercise time aside for yourself. And when your 10th exercise anniversary comes along at the turn of the century, give me a call, and we'll celebrate your wellness success together.

Health, like wealth, is a gift. We must earn and preserve both. Be sensitive to how your workplace impacts mental and physical health. Lead by example. Commit to leading through a healthful personal lifestyle. And be protective of the health needs of your associates.

FUTURISTIC HABIT 2

What You Dream Is What You Get

"Our aspirations are our possibilities."
— *Robert Browning*

"If you don't have a vision of it, you won't get it." "You've got to see it before you can be it." Cliches? Yes. Accurate? You bet.

In 1975 my wife, Lynne, first spoke of her attraction to the Rocky Mountains—sharing that some day she would like to have a mountain home. We talked about it frequently from then on.

Ten years later, while in Colorado for a summer vacation, we decided to look at some property. We wanted to do some homework on what had by then become a vision of everyone in our family. We went to several open houses and absorbed a lot of information. The Colorado resort areas were in the middle of a serious property recession in the mid '80s, which gave us all the more desire to check out opportunities.

Our eyes were bigger than our pocketbook. We couldn't afford our vision in 1985, but the family knew we had a Colorado destiny. We were preparing.

It was during this trip that we first visited a new Summit County development called Summerwood. It was both beautiful and expensive—far too expensive for the Byrne family. We put Summerwood into the fantasy column. Maybe someday.

Six months later, following a day's skiing, we visited an open house at a new development called Watch Hill. It had an inviting, panoramic mountain view, one of our priorities. Again, we couldn't justify spending what they were asking, but we liked what we saw.

The Watch Hill unit we first looked at in February, 1986, was still new and unoccupied a year later. The price had come down, but not enough for our budget. We once again left Colorado with nothing but our vision of Watch Hill and our fantasy of Summerwood. We were sure the Watch Hill unit would sell before we were ready.

We returned to Colorado again in August, 1987, for a brief vacation. We decided to rent a condo at the Watch Hill development we first saw 18 months earlier. On a whim, just a couple of days before going home, we decided to see if the corner unit we had looked at and liked was still for sale. We found it was—and at a substantially reduced price.

The price change was so dramatic we couldn't pass it up. We bought our small condo at Watch Hill for a full 40 percent less than the price only 18 months earlier. While thoroughly enjoying our new mountain home at Watch Hill, we continued to play out our fantasy by returning every year or so to monitor the activities at Summerwood.

The Byrne foursome visited Summerwood again in July, 1990, "just driving through." To our surprise, we saw an open house sign, so we walked in. We quickly got reacquainted with realtor Eddie O'Brien, who greeted us with "year after year after year." Eddie obviously remembered the Byrne family. He gave us a quick update.

The property, sitting on a ridge 300 feet above Lake Dillon, was almost sold out. God wasn't going to make more of it. Our motivation was high. It looked like a now or never situation. We stretched our minds and our pocketbook. Before the day was over our fantasy came true. The wondrous view I had literally dreamed of over the past five years now belonged to my family.

That evening Jason, Jenny, Lynne, and I sat down to discuss what makes dreams come true and how twice in three years we were at the right place at the right time. We concluded we had done our homework and had gathered substantial market knowledge. We also concluded that opportunity most often visits the prepared mind.

I used to think everything I heard about imagery, visualization, and dreams coming true was a bunch of baloney. In recent years, however, my personal experience has proven I don't attain goals I don't have, and I don't fulfill dreams I don't dream. Our Colorado home is a testament to the value of dreaming the improbable dream.

Our future will be as bright as we visualize it to be, or as dull as no vision at all. Good things really don't just happen. What we achieve is limited only by what we are able to visualize. We've got to see it before we can have it.

FUTURISTIC HABIT 3

The Risk/Reward Relation-ship. Constantly Re-defined. Constantly Revised.

When entrepreneurial achievers build their better mousetraps they frequently put everything on the line. Young, gutsy, let's-go-for-it achievers are our economy's strongest allies. Everything begins somewhere, and the entrepreneurial person is often the spark plug. With entrepreneurial success comes monetary reward, which in turn changes the Risk/Reward Relationship.

An entrepreneurial friend sold his company at age 52 for almost five million dollars. It was the first time in his life he really had any excess cash. He and his wife stayed in the Midwest for a year, then moved permanently to Arizona. He had stars in his eyes and money in his pocket. The stars stayed. The money didn't.

Even though certificates of deposit would have been just fine, he wanted to show Arizona how to develop property. Unfortunately, he ran into some folks who wanted to help him, or so he thought. He became involved in about every quick-buck real estate deal south of Flagstaff. When prices plunged shortly afterward, he came close to losing everything but his underwear. He was able to hold on long enough for his real estate to partially rebound, then escaped with enough to keep the college tuition promise he made to his grandkids—and just enough to retire on.

What did my friend do wrong? He made two major errors. The first was becoming involved in a business he had no experience in. The second error, and the more significant one, was in not re-defining and revising his risk parameters—a requirement issued him on the day he accepted his multi-million dollar check.

Acceptable risk levels are not constant. They change every time one's financial position changes. Oddly, they change in a direction opposite the prevailing wisdom.

It appears at first glance that the more money you have the more risk you can take. True and false. True because the absolute amount you can put at risk increases as assets increase. And false because increased assets give us more to protect. While the absolute amount put at risk may be greater, the amount as a percentage of personal wealth should become increasingly smaller. That's what my Arizona friend forgot—he went south with a bagful of money and put it all at risk in leveraged, highly speculative ventures.

Pure financial theory suggests that risk doesn't exist when assets aren't at risk. Theoretically, therefore, risk increases as wealth increases.

What level of debt can you responsibly afford to assume? There are three answers:

1) A debt predictably covered by personal earnings.

2) A debt that will fund itself by way of increased cash flow.

3) A debt that is offset by savings or other ready cash.

Assuming leverage beyond that, especially by someone with considerable assets, is not advisable.

The more wealth you have, the more conservative you should be when analyzing what percentage of it to put at risk. Again, the absolute amount may increase, but as wealth increases, the relation-ship of at-risk funds to total assets should consistently be reduced.

The three R's: Risk to Reward Relationship—is one relation-ship that should always be changing.

FUTURISTIC HABIT 4

Speaking of Your Success

"It usually takes more than three weeks to prepare a good impromptu speech."

— *Mark Twain*

Listen up. If you are an achieving leader your time to speak is coming.

For 15 years I have listed my occupation as entrepreneur. And for 15 years I have maintained a JIC (just in case) file. It includes dictated thoughts, beliefs and impressions, philosophies important to me, futuristic trends I envision, and highlights of reading material I want to remember. My JIC file also includes items and perspectives I thought would someday be of interest to others when I spoke to them.

There are three types of speakers. The first type make their living speaking, but have never had the benefit of living their subject matter. They live off the entertaining anecdote and manufactured drama. They speak glibly, tell a few good stories, arouse your interest sporadically and momentarily, collect their check, and move on to the next town to repeat their *schtik* to another group. They leave little of value behind.

The second type of speaker may or may not speak professionally but knows the subject from personal experience because he or she has lived it. This speaker has an impact on the audience because of credibility, as well as acceptable platform presence. The primary motivation to speak is to share personal experiences.

There is a passion for the topic, and it shows. When leaving the room he or she leaves something behind that the audience can chew on.

The third speaker type speaks for profit but also offers topical depth and value to the audience. Many celebrity executives and authors fall into this classification.

If you are like me, many speakers have let you down. More often than not, the letdown came from those who didn't have credibility and personal experience within their subject area. Often, the speaker had stage presence and a glib delivery. He or she may or may not be making a good living, but it's all the person knows how to do, so he or she speaks as much as possible. This speaker proves you don't need impact to make a living speaking.

Here you come, a successful achiever. People want to know what you do and how you do it. They ask you to give a talk. Have no fear. With practice and preparation, you can give a better speech than many of the so-called pros. I would rather listen to a thoughtful, organized, and prepared business person fresh from the firing line any day. And so would most others.

How do you handle the transition from desk to platform? I don't pass it off as easy, but it's certainly not impossible.

Helpful Tips for the Beginning Speaker

Talk only on a topic you have a passion for. If the words aren't in your heart, keep them off your lips. Your passion will show in living color. A lack of it is cause to stay seated.

Organize material chronologically, by category, and by contrast. Gather two or more points that play off of each other.

Prepare, prepare more, then prepare some more. Use a video camera or mirror. Rehearse repeatedly.

Work extra hard on the first five minutes of your talk. Know what you want to say, including something humorous. It doesn't have to be a knee slapper. Do what you are comfortable with.

Change the pace every 10 minutes or so. Lighten up the message, tell about a real-life experience or back off the heavy stuff at least briefly. This "change up" will maintain their attention.

Rehearse your message so you don't need to read a script. Use notes with key topical and transitional words instead.

Write your own introduction. Too many introducers either get carried away or hardly say anything. Write an introduction and ask the introducer to read it word for word. Note: The best speakers with the strongest credentials often have the shortest introductions. Don't get carried away with your own importance.

Do not try to psych the audience. This is a technique of motivational speakers. Audiences are moving away from motivation and toward harder-edged content.

Be yourself. Don't try to con the audience. Be comfortable with yourself. Find a way to get the audience to participate. You may want them to vote on something by raising their hand, standing up to stretch, etc. Create physical participation.

Use visual aids cautiously. Too many visual aids are both confusing and distracting. Be sure they can be clearly seen from the back of the room. Don't produce them on a typewriter.

Spend time with the audience before you talk. It will loosen you up, and you will feel a rapport before you begin.

Use a microphone. Don't let a small audience fool you. It's the size and type of room that's important, not the number of people.

Move your body. Don't hide behind the podium. You may not be comfortable at first without a podium, but at least step away from it briefly every few minutes. Gesture occasionally.

Alter your voice. Change pitch and pace frequently. Combine this with body movement.

Be sensitive to eye contact. Look at specific people on all sides and at all distances. Stay beaded on one person for at least three seconds at a time, then move to someone else.

Assume a wide stance. A narrow stance is weak and sissified. A wide stance transmits authority.

Ask provocative questions. Cause the audience to think. You may ask rhetorically, or you may want to use questions as a way to get the audience physically involved. Either way, it's effective.

Include short, crisp sentences. This provides a change of pace that adds emphasis and impact.

End with emphasis. Opportunities include going back over key points in summary form, asking the audience to take action, or ending with an anecdote, quotation, or humor. Conclude with something that really charges you up and excites you. It will do the same for the audience.

FUTURISTIC HABIT 5

A Special Way to Give Something Back

Achievement opens the door to many opportunities others don't have. Among them is the probability that our experiences will add depth to our perspective. When we practice our vocation seriously, continuously investing in our intellectual capital, we enrich our mind as well as our pocketbook. Growing knowledge and success provide increased self-confidence in our abilities—confidence that we have something to offer, something to say. And something to give.

There comes a natural, transitional time when many achievers begin to divert part of their attention away from themselves and their business and toward others. That attention takes many forms. We can give money, and we do. But we can give in another important way—we can give of ourselves. Sharing what is in your mind may be the greatest gift of all.

Giving to Education

Every employer knows the basic skills of workers entering the workplace is declining. Spelling, writing a decent letter, punctuality, and reliability are basics becoming more scarce. The problem, and remedy, is partly in our educational system.

During the 1980s we worked to improve teacher pay, stiffen graduation requirements and update physical facilities. It isn't working.

The growth of private schools also continued in the '80s. Many of the best elementary and secondary schools in America are now private. They have grown and excelled in spite of often paying teachers less than public schools, in spite of spending less to educate each student than public schools and in spite of having class sizes similar to public schools. What gives?

Here's a magazine column I wrote in May, 1990:

I'd like your opinion. Your vote, actually. The issue is important, especially in May.

May is cap and gown month, graduation time. The time when graduates finally get an opportunity to "walk their talk." We go to the commencement and, more often than not, listen to a speaker that motivates the graduate about as much as a car with a rusty rocker panel. We eat the cake, drink the coffee, read the cards, count the money, and give our best wishes.

When the smiling is over and tears have gone, we return to our parental world, assured that Terry and Teresa Terrific received a great elementary and secondary education and are ready for college or career. Really?

I'm not so sure. More and more, we're graduating students to a workplace they're not prepared for. At The Byrne Companies we take the basic skills like writing and spelling seriously. We're one of the few businesses that gives a spelling test to all employment applicants.

Frequently, the results provide us doubt about our educators. One applicant stands out in my mind. He had recently graduated from Iowa State. He flunked our spelling test miserably. I remember asking, "Ron, how could you graduate from a great school like Iowa State and not be able to spell?" He bravely looked me square in the eye and said, "Mr. Byrne, it's a shame, isn't it."

To get a high school diploma in Japan, the student needs six years of English. In America, only one high school graduate in 500 has had three years of Japanese.

In 1989, the budget of the training program at IBM was greater than the entire budget of Harvard. Motorola says that between 20 and 40 percent of its applicants fail math and English tests written at the seventh to ninth grade level. And we're supposed to compete in a world economy?

It seems when we discuss the quality of education we talk money. More likely we're talking teacher pay. Remember the vote I asked for? Well, it's related to money, too. Imagine that you're asked to vote yes or no on the following question: *Are teachers underpaid?*

My answer: *Yes they are, and no they aren't.*

As in other occupations, we can point to teachers that are terrific and to others who are terrible. Unlike most other occupations, however, teachers aren't effectively measured. The marginal ones make the same money as the excellent ones. That's the real problem with American education. And that's why some teachers make too much, and others make too little.

Our good teachers are seriously underpaid. Yes, it's time we did something about it. But first, we need some help from the teachers. We need their participation in finding ways to determine who the great teachers are so we can financially reward them.

It's not the taxpayer who's holding back teacher pay. It's the system—a system that insists at contract time that all teachers are created equal. They're not.

When teachers gain the courage to be measured, our classrooms will come alive with excitement and creativity. Our graduates will be better prepared to make their contribution. And our taxpayers will respond with the additional money that the great teachers so thoroughly deserve.

And I'll be at the front of the line.

For years, America has been trying to *buy* better education. It hasn't worked. And it won't.

There are three missing links. The first, as the magazine column suggests, is teacher measurement. We need to bring our educators into the free enterprise, supply-and-demand fold. We must find a way to reward teachers on the basis of achievement. The only way it can be done is to develop and install measurement criteria.

The second missing link isn't in our schools, it's in our homes. We've made parents out of too many teachers. Classroom time is used to provide discipline that is the responsibility of parents. More working mothers and more broken marriages translate to less parental involvement. These trends burden our schools and teachers. Parents aren't playing a strong role in public education. American education will stay on the ropes until they do.

Why are private schools increasingly providing better educations with less money? A large reason is parental involvement. Simply put, parents who send their offspring to private schools are more engrossed in their children's education.

The third missing link in education is the business community. The private sector of our economy employs more graduates than any other group of employers. Yet finding, even occasionally, a high school teacher who really understands and enthusiastically supports our free enterprise system is difficult. More often, they are victims of what they hear on the evening news or read in their newspaper—a superficial account of corporate mischief. That is not the free enterprise system I know, the one that exists in the real world.

Giving of ourselves to students is a very special and uniquely important contribution. Today's students, especially at the high school level, lack role models. They go to school and spend most of their time with teachers who know as much about entrepreneurship and achievement as I know about molecular biology. While molecular biology will never be important to me, odds are good the world of business, entrepreneurship, and achievement will be extremely important to many students.

Students need firsthand, front row opportunities to discuss risk-taking, the fear of failure, business ethics, and the realities of the marketplace. They aren't getting that opportunity, and I'm fearful they won't until the business community gets involved in the classroom. Our school administrators have been remiss in not asking for business involvement. The business community has been even more remiss in not advocating it.

Does your community have a school-business partnership? How about Junior Achievement? If so, get involved. Or tell your school administrators you are ready to volunteer time to one or more interested students.

Our American educational system isn't merely behind. It's lost. We need involvement from the business community to help get it back on track.

The next time an educator tells you we can solve our educational problem with what's inside our pocketbooks, pleasantly but firmly disagree. And do something more. Offer to go to his or her school and give some of what's inside your head. Offer your perspective and life experience.

Give of your mind—a very special kind of educational giving.

Giving As a Mentor

Mentoring is typically a one-on-one relationship between a mentor and a protege. It can also be a group activity between a mentor and two or more mentees.

A mentor relationship is based on the desire of one party to seek counsel from another, coupled with the willingness of the other party to freely and unselfishly give it. That sounds like a one-way proposition, but it isn't. Both parties win.

The mentor-mentee or mentor-protege relationship occurs between someone identified as "senior" and one or more others considered "junior." An effective mentor relationship builds trust between the parties, facilitates effective communication, and encourages both formal and informal interaction. The relationship often involves a specific interest area but can also be general in nature.

Mentoring is more than an opportunity. When you make a mentoring commitment it's a responsibility. As in other areas of your professional life, expectations are reality. So don't make promises you won't keep.

Effective, helpful mentors are available as agreed and aren't on a pedestal. On the contrary, they approach mentoring with a disposition not only to teach but also to learn. They consider their knowledge less than perfect and are dedicated to continued learning.

Mentees and proteges also make a commitment—to be serious about personal growth, about maintaining inquisitiveness, and about being appreciative of the mentor's contribution. The road runs both ways.

Is the greatest gift we can give in our pocketbook? Or is it in our mind? Support our future by looking for ways to share your intellectual capital with students.

FUTURISTIC HABIT 6

Read, Read, Read

Nothing is as powerful as knowledge. Other than our hands-on experiences, there's no better way to get knowledge than reading.

I have the 15/15 plan going for me. For the last 15 years I have dedicated more than 15 hours weekly to nonfiction reading—all outside office hours.

Reading, like listening, is an excellent way to inhale information. As you develop your future strategies and directions, consider allocating part of your day and week to broadening your knowledge base. Invest in yourself. It's rewarding, fun, and profitable.

FUTURISTIC HABIT 7

The Three Levels of Joy

"What lies behind us and what lies before us are tiny matters compared to what lies within us."
— *Ralph Waldo Emerson*

Father Tom Mosher, former pastor of St. Mary's Church in Breckenridge, Colorado, is a terrific communicator. My vision of an ideal future was impacted by a talk he gave on the three levels of joy.

"Oh" Joy

The first level of joy is something unexpected and unplanned, yet pleasant and warm. If your mate gives you a spontaneous kiss, if your son or daughter shows you a report card with better grades than you expected, or if someone gives you a surprise pat on the back or pays a compliment, you say "Oh, how nice." Something kind, generous, and at least mildly surprising—that's "Oh" joy. And it feels good.

"Alleluia" Joy

The second level of joy results from a sense of "mission accomplished." When we graduate from college, have our first child, complete an important professional objective, or get elected to an important office we experience a sense of significance—the sense of completion that accompanies "Alleluia" joy. It is less fleeting than "Oh" joy, lasting longer, and makes a more permanent impression.

"Amen" Joy

"Amen" is the third and highest level of the joy experience, and while not as common as "Oh" and "Alleluia," is more permanently fulfilling.

We achieve "Amen" when we arrive at a place of personal comfort and satisfaction with our life and how we have lived it. "Amen" is an internal and eternal joy. A happy marriage for ourselves or those close to us, children living within our intended ethical and moral boundaries, knowing ourselves and being at peace with who we are and what we have been—all are signs of "Amen" joy.

Professionally, the experience of "Amen" joy might include satisfaction derived from developing people or organizations, opportunities we created for others, or watching our successor perform faithfully within the norms of behavior we nurtured. The feeling of "Amen" joy is deep, warm, and everlasting. It is the level of joy allowed by our conscience.

As we look ahead, let's contemplate how we can structure our achievement so some day our conscience allows us to look back and say, "Amen."

FUTURISTIC HABIT 8

Have You Made Your Life's Choices?

"Choice, not chance, determines destiny."

Habits of Wealth is a product of many year's preparation, even though I had no plans to write a book. I was preparing myself, in many different ways, to achieve effectively. I maintained files of ideas and concepts important to me. I dictated personal notes. I grew through listening, reading, assimilating information at seminars, and practicing leadership in the best way I knew how. Only because of this preparation did I come to believe there was a book in me. Even then, it took some unexpected but motivating encouragement before I committed to it.

My motivation for writing *Habits of Wealth* is to give something back, to share an entrepreneurial philosophy I believe in and care about deeply. I hope it will have a positive impact on people through personal and organizational prosperity.

I've had many positive entrepreneurial experiences. However, I believe my greatest accomplishment is the wholeness of my life experience. I enjoy my entrepreneurial life tremendously. I've developed a self-knowledge that success and achievement are more important than one's financial statement. Life's measurement is not only quantitative but qualitative.

At a New Year's Eve party in 1986, friend Mark Jerstad asked me what I thought I'd be doing in five years. I vividly remember the question, a profound one for an entrepreneur constantly evaluating ideas and opportunities. For some reason, I had an immediate answer, one that just came to me. I said, "I don't know, Mark . . . isn't that great?"

That doesn't sound like it came from a fellow who prides himself in disciplined organizational planning, does it? Nonetheless, my response was accurate. I didn't know then, and I don't know today what I'll be doing in five years. If I knew, it would betray my entrepreneurship.

It turns out that Mark didn't know, either. He has since realized a lifelong professional dream. He is now CEO of the Good Samaritan Society.

Although I was proud to say that New Year's Eve I didn't know what I wanted to be doing in five years, I did know the answer to a more important question: What I wanted *to be* in five years.

My greatest accomplishment isn't what I've done. It's what I've been. And what I've been is the same as what I want *to be*. It's the anchor of knowing what I want *to be* that gives me the freedom to choose what I want *to do*.

There are two sides to an enriched entrepreneurial life. One is an active *to be* identity. *To be* provides boundaries of thought and activity within which the other side—our *to do* side—makes its choices. *To be* is the conscience of *to do*. An organization has neither ethics nor conscience. That comes from its leader, who either enriches or damages the quality of the enterprise through the *to be* model.

The higher your ladder takes you, the more important it becomes that your *to be* priorities are in writing. Here are mine—what I want *to be*. I call them My Life's Choices.

MY LIFE'S CHOICES

I choose the risk of achieving great things within well-defined ethical boundaries, and to forego achievement that compromises those boundaries.

I choose to lead my life rather than let life lead me.

I choose the willingness to hold courageous points of view, and accept responsibility for any consequences.

I choose to activate, as well as participate; to decide, not just contemplate; to seek—not merely accept—change.

I choose to have vision, doing today what will provide my family, associates, and customers with opportunities and growth tomorrow.

I choose to nurture, support, and advocate courageous, ethical entrepreneurship at every opportunity—believing from it will flow our greatest achievements.

I choose above all to be a caring, loving husband and father, responsible for balanced priorities and value-based leadership.

Formal, written planning helps to create success for an organization. It's similarly true that formalizing your personal choices can create personal success. Do yourself a favor. Think about what you want *to be*. Then commit your choices to writing.

FUTURISTIC HABIT 9

The Entrepreneur's Credo

In 1986, the American Entrepreneurs Association published the *Entrepreneur's Credo*. It is a courageous statement about those who choose to be daring participants in free enterprise. Its words hold important meaning for entrepreneurial achievers. I can't think of a better way to end a chapter on your future than to ask you to contemplate its message.

ENTREPRENEUR'S CREDO

"I do not choose to be a common person. It is my right to be uncommon—if I can. I seek opportunity—not security. I do not wish to be a kept citizen, humbled and dulled by having the state look after me.

I want to take the calculated risk, to dream and to build, to fail and to succeed.

I refuse to barter incentive for a dole; I prefer the challenges of life to the guaranteed existence: the thrill of fulfillment to the stale calm of Utopia.

I will not trade my freedom for beneficence nor my dignity for a handout. I will never cower before any master nor bend to any threat.

It is my heritage to stand erect, proud and unafraid; to think and act for myself, to enjoy the benefit of my creations and to face the world boldly and say:

This with God's help, I have done. All this is what it means to be an Entrepreneur."

Official Credo of American Entrepreneurs Association © 1986

Bill Byrne

IX

PLANNING FOR PERMANENT PROSPERITY

"If you are not making the progress you would like to make and are capable of making, it is simply because your goals are not clearly defined."
— *Paul J. Meyer*

While this chapter is at the back of the book, you should position your understanding of planning toward the *front* of your business career. Your commitment to planning is fundamentally important to creating and preserving personal and organizational wealth.

PLANNING HABIT 1

Giving Scrutiny to Your Business Continuity

In 1979 a young insurance agent representing New York Life called on me. He didn't come with answers, but with questions. Before our half-hour meeting was over, Steve Garry had made quite an impression on me.

When, a few years later, I was ready to aggressively update my personal and business planning, I called Steve. Since then we have turned a lot of sod, looking for opportunities to prepare for tomorrow.

Steve's creative and informed approach to business and personal planning has distinguished him as a consistent member of the Summit Group, a group which includes only the top 100 agents among the more than 12,000 representing New York Life. He has not only helped in the organization of this Habit, but we have implemented every wealth-creating suggestion discussed. To us, "giving scrutiny to your business continuity" isn't an academic exercise—it's a real life opportunity.

If you want to be an achiever, it's emphatically important that you plan. If you're already successful, the planning recommendations in this chapter are powerful enough to create significant wealth for you.

If you have a business partner or partners, a Business Continuity Agreement is as important a business document as you will ever put your pen to. If you don't have a partner, the selective planning techniques described here will still be highly useful, though applied somewhat differently.

Essentially, a Business Continuity Agreement keeps the company in the hands the owners wish. For the shareholder leaving the business, it provides a predetermined value and a waiting market. It also stipulates the terms of stock transfer and under what conditions a buyout is to take place.

Would you like it if you were forced into business with your partner's spouse? How about an ex-spouse? Or how about the partner's child? Worse yet, your partner's five children, who were each willed 20 percent of your former partner's ownership? Even if you don't have a partner, dying without a stipulation of value may result in an expensive encounter with the IRS. The only way to avoid the consequences of the above illustrations is by having an up-to-date Business Continuity Agreement.

Selecting the Right Agreement

There are two types of agreements. One is the *Cross-Purchase* (Diagram B), which provides for the remaining shareholder(s) to purchase the departing shareholder's stock. The second type of agreement—the *Stock Redemption* Agreement (Diagram C) stipulates the corporation will buy the departing owner's stock.

Both agreements are activated by a shareholder's death. The agreement obligates the estate of the deceased to sell its stock to either the remaining stockholders or the company. It also commits the continuing shareholders or the company, depending on the type of contract, to purchase all stock held by the estate.

There are several circumstances, in addition to death, that would activate a properly designed and funded Business Continuity Agreement. They include:

Shareholder disability

Shareholder reaching an agreed upon retirement age

Voluntary retirement

Involuntary termination

Business disagreements

Transfer required by divorce

Transfer required by personal bankruptcy of shareholder

Miscellaneous—any reason legally set in agreement

Selecting the Right Professionals

To select and create the right agreement for your situation you will need an attorney specifically experienced in estate planning. Since life and disability insurance usually fund an effective agreement, you will also need an insurance agent, preferably a Chartered Life Underwriter (CLU) and/or a Chartered Financial Consultant (ChFC). Insurance provides the funds to buy stock when the agreement is activated by one of the above circumstances or by death.

Be careful in your agent selection. Find an agent with documented planning experience. Many simply aren't qualified to handle this type of sophisticated need.

The agent and lawyer you choose should be asked to provide references that he or she is well versed in business insurance.

Selecting the Right Insurance Company

Question: If you buy a million dollar life insurance policy and the insurance company comes upon tough times, how much do you have at risk? The total premiums paid? The total premiums paid plus the cost of acquiring new coverage at your current age and health? Or a million dollars? The worst case answer is a million dollars, which could become reality if your timing was unfortunate.

Never has the risk been so great you might outlive your insurance company. Therefore, never has the selection of an insurance carrier been so important.

Major U.S. media markets are seeing and hearing unusual advertising messages these days. "If being exciting means investing heavily in junk bonds that end up in default," a New York Life ad says, "that's the kind of excitement we can all do without." Guardian Life ads boast, "No junk bonds? No junk real estate? No kidding!" Selecting the right insurance company is more complex than buying the cheapest or highest return policy you can get from a friend, neighbor, or relative. A whole lot more complex.

We have heard of the many troubled life and property insurers searching for capital infusions, merger partners, and other forms of private financing to get them out of jeopardy. We're looking at the tip of an iceberg that will affect us for years to come.

DIAGRAM B

Buy/Sell Agreement
(Cross Purchase Plan)

```
$ $ $ $ $ $ $ $ $ $              $ $ $ $ $ $ $ $ $ $ $
$                 $              $                   $
$ Stockholder "A" $ - - Premiums - ->  $   Insurance    $
$                 $              $    Company       $
$ $ $ $ $ $ $ $ $ $              $ $ $ $ $ $ $ $ $ $ $
```

For Policy on Life Stockholder "B";
Policy Values Owned by Stockholder "A."

At Death of Stockholder "B":

```
$ $ $ $ $ $ $ $ $ $
$                 $
$   Insurance     $
$   Company       $
$ $ $ $ $ $ $ $ $ $  Income Tax-Free
                  - - Proceeds - ->  $ $ $ $ $ $ $ $ $ $ $
                                     $                   $
                                     $ Stockholder "A"   $
                       Pays Insurance $                   $
$ $ $ $ $ $ $ $ $ $  <- - Proceeds - -  $ $ $ $ $ $ $ $ $ $ $
$                 $
$   Estate of     $
$ Stockholder "B" $
$                 $  Sells Stock
$ $ $ $ $ $ $ $ $ $- - - - - at - - - - ->$ $ $ $ $ $ $ $ $ $ $
                   Established Price  $                   $
                                     $ Stockholder "A"   $
                                     $                   $
                                     $ $ $ $ $ $ $ $ $ $ $
```

DIAGRAM C

Buy/Sell Agreement
(Stock Redemption Plan)

```
$ $ $ $ $ $ $ $ $ $              $ $ $ $ $ $ $ $ $ $ $
$                 $              $                   $
$ Aggressive, Inc. $ - - Premiums - -> $   Insurance  $
$                 $              $    Company        $
$ $ $ $ $ $ $ $ $ $              $ $ $ $ $ $ $ $ $ $ $
```

For Policy on Life of Each Stockholder;
Policy Values Owned by Aggressive, Inc.

At Death of Any Stockholder:

```
$ $ $ $ $ $ $ $ $ $
$                 $
$   Insurance     $
$   Company       $
$                 $    Income Tax-Free
$ $ $ $ $ $ $ $ $ $    - - Proceeds - ->   $ $ $ $ $ $ $ $ $ $ $
                                           $                   $
                                           $ Aggressive, Inc.  $
$ $ $ $ $ $ $ $ $ $    Pays Insurance      $                   $
$                 $    <- - Proceeds - -   $ $ $ $ $ $ $ $ $ $ $
$ Estate of Deceased $
$   Stockholder    $
$                 $    Sells Stock
$ $ $ $ $ $ $ $ $ $    - - - - at - - - ->  $ $ $ $ $ $ $ $ $ $ $
                      Established Price      $                   $
                                             $ Aggressive, Inc.  $
                                             $                   $
                                             $ $ $ $ $ $ $ $ $ $ $
```

Today, when we pick someone to insure our future, we better do it as though our financial life depended on it—because it does.

Twenty-two billion dollars in corporate bonds defaulted in 1990, and the Bond Investors Association projected $25 billion more in 1991. According to a study prepared by an American Express division and reported by Bill Sing in the *Los Angeles Times*, there is "significant risk" that a severe economic downturn or decline in major investment markets could result in the insolvency of one-fifth of the nation's major life insurers! How can we avoid this historically significant investment trap?

First of all, don't rely on your insurance salesperson's opinion. Second, remember there is no such thing as extra yield without extra risk. Third, and most important, check what the rating services say. Three primary services rate insurance company financial strength—Moody's, Standard and Poor, and A. M. Best.

Moody's recently rated 71 North American life insurers and gave their highest AAA rating to only 17. During the same period, Standard and Poor rated 103 North American companies and gave their highest AAA rating to 40. A. M. Best, the "gentler and kinder" rating service who—unlike the others— rates only insurance companies, recently gave their top A+ (Superior) rating to 259 insurers. Also unlike the others, Best has 15 Financial Size Categories ranging from policyholder surplus reserves of one million dollars, all the way up to two billion plus.

While the above statistics are helpful, selecting the right insurer can still be a confusing task. So let's get to the bottom line. Of the more than 1,000 companies ready to sell you life insurance, only six hold the highest rating from all three rating agencies. Among companies with two billion or more in surplus reserves there are only four: Metropolitan Life, New York Life, Northwestern Mutual, and Teachers Insurance and Annuity. Other companies qualifying among the elite are State Farm and Guardian. The list is shrinking. Twelve months earlier twice as many companies made this increasingly hallowed list.

Your choice of an insurance carrier to fund your personal and business planning will impact your life for a long time. When I chose Steve Garry and New York Life several years ago, the junk bond alarm hadn't yet sounded. Nonetheless, Steve and I talked about these questions at length. When you have millions of insurance dollars on the line as I have, quality and security become important words. I was sensitive to quality because I knew everything in life has a cycle and that someday my diligence might be important. That day has already come.

The Situation

Five years ago you and a partner started Aggressive, Inc. Since then, business has been good and your Business Continuity Agreement carries a $1 million valuation. You fund the agreement with two $500,000 life insurance policies—one on the life of each partner.

Funding Alternatives

Before we examine agreements in detail, let's review the four alternatives that exist to create the cash necessary to buy out a deceased partner's $500,000 interest in Aggressive, Inc. The costs associated with these various alternatives are shown in Diagram D.

Funding Alternative 1: Borrowing $500,000 at the time of a partner's death may be difficult. Credit positions often change when an owner dies. Nonetheless, as Diagram D shows, if a loan was available at 10 percent and repaid over a 10 year period, the cost to create $500,000 would be $813,727. It costs $1.62 to create each dollar.

Funding Alternative 2: Aggressive, Inc.'s corporate surplus might provide the cash necessary to buy out the deceased partner's interest, but it's not likely. An active and growing company doesn't retain large cash reserves. However, if the cash *were* available in corporate surplus, the second graph on Diagram D illustrates that each dollar costs one dollar. That is without any tax considerations.

Funding Alternative 3: The alternative of term insurance may be appropriate and practical in the very early years of a company. Eventually, however, the cost becomes prohibitive. The need for cash is permanent; term insurance is only a temporary solution. As Diagram D shows, the cost of term premiums to create a $500,000 death benefit for a 40-year-old male living to life expectancy is $477,740.

Funding Alternative 4: The permanent life insurance alternative, shown on the right of Diagram D, allows a business owner to create significant benefits payable at death. As the graph illustrates, the total premium outlay to create a paid-up $500,000 permanent policy is $77,900. Premium payments are required for only 10 years. Death benefits would, however, remain intact until death. The cost to create a dollar through permanent insurance? Less than 16 cents.

Clearly, the long-term view supports funding by permanent insurance.

Agreement Alternatives

In most cases, the Cross-Purchase agreement is the preferred instrument over the Stock Redemption agreement. While both have equal legal integrity, the Cross-Purchase has tax advantages at death.

A Stock Redemption agreement, on the other hand, may be advantageous when multiple shareholders are involved. For example, if ten shareholders were considering an agreement, it would be more convenient to have a single buyer in the event of death, i.e. the corporation under a Stock Redemption agreement.

The following example for Aggressive, Inc. depicts scenarios for both agreements:

Stock Redemption

When your partner dies, the company receives tax-free insurance proceeds of $500,000 and pays it to your partner's estate to buy the stock. Assuming you each paid in $10,000 when Aggressive, Inc. was formed, and you later sold it for $1,000,000, you would have a capital gain of $990,000.

DIAGRAM D

Aggressive, Inc.

Alternatives to Create $500,000 for the Purchase of a Deceased Partner's Interest

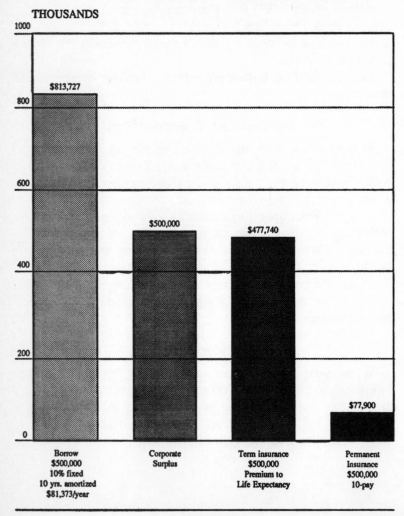

THOUSANDS

$813,727	Borrow $500,000 10% fixed 10 yrs. amortized $81,373/year
$500,000	Corporate Surplus
$477,740	Term insurance $500,000 Premium to Life Expectancy
$77,900	Permanent Insurance $500,000 10-pay

Cross-Purchase

When your partner dies, you (not the company) receive the tax-free $500,000 insurance proceeds to buy the stock. If you later sold Aggressive, Inc. for the same $1,000,000 as above, you would reduce your capital gain by $500,000 to $490,000 (versus $990,000). All you did to reduce the capital gain liability was structure the Business Continuation Agreement as a Cross-Purchase (so the surviving stockholder was responsible to buy the stock) rather than a Stock Redemption (where the corporation buys the stock).

The tax impact on your partner's survivor is the same under both agreements—the estate receives the $500,000 income tax free. The savings occur at the time of the next sale. The Cross-Purchase structure "steps up" the cost basis $500,000 by permitting the surviving owner to use a cost basis of $510,000 rather than looking all the way back to when Aggressive, Inc. began, with a per-shareholder cost of $10,000.

The "stepped-up" cost basis is the primary reason the Cross-Purchase agreement is often favored over the Stock Redemption agreement. But circumstances vary. That is why you need expert legal and insurance counsel.

The Splendor of Split-Dollar

Business owners naturally prefer that the business pays the insurance premium from corporate funds, rather than taking it from personal funds. The IRS would frown on this arrangement were it not for another concept, thought by many to be the most appropriate companion to business continuity planning. It's called Split Dollar (Diagram E). The concept of Split Dollar is more appropriate for a C corporation. In an S corporation, the concept referred to as Executive Bonus is usually better.

Split Dollar uses business dollars to help owners obtain personal insurance and cash benefits on a favored basis, even if it only involves one shareholder. However, let's continue to assume there are two partner-owners.

DIAGRAM E

Split Dollar Insurance
(Collateral Assignment Approach)

```
$ $ $ $ $ $ $ $ $ $ $ $ $ $                    $ $ $ $ $ $ $ $ $ $ $ $ $ $
$                          $                    $                        $
$   Aggressive, Inc.       $- - - - - Premiums - - - - ->$   Insurance    $
$                          $                    $       Company          $
$ $ $ $ $ $ $ $ $ $ $ $ $ $                    $ $ $ $ $ $ $ $ $ $ $ $ $ $
```

Partner A is owner and beneficiary of policy on Partner B. Partner A makes collateral assignment to Aggressive, Inc. which may use policy values at any time and receive full return of premiums paid at Partner B's death.

```
                                              $ $ $ $ $ $ $ $ $ $ $ $ $ $
                                              $                        $
At Death of Partner B:                        $     Aggressive, Inc.   $
                              Income Tax-Free  $                       $
$ $ $ $ $ $ $ $ $ $ $ $ $ $ $ $- - - - - Proceeds - - - - ->$ $ $ $ $ $ $ $ $ $ $ $ $ $
$                            $  Equal to Premiums Paid
$        Insurance           $
$        Company             $
$                            $  Income Tax-Free
$ $ $ $ $ $ $ $ $ $ $ $ $ $ $ $- - - - - Proceeds - - - - ->$ $ $ $ $ $ $ $ $ $ $ $ $ $
                              Equal to Remainder of  $                  $
                                  Policy             $    Partner A      $
                                                     $                  $
                                              $ $ $ $ $ $ $ $ $ $ $ $ $ $
```

Partner A complies with Business Continuity Agreement.

```
                                              $ $ $ $ $ $ $ $ $ $ $ $ $ $
                                              $                        $
At Retirement of Partner B:                   $     Aggressive, Inc.   $
                              Income Tax-Free  $                       $
$ $ $ $ $ $ $ $ $ $ $ $ $ $ $ $- Repayment of Premium ->$ $ $ $ $ $ $ $ $ $ $ $ $ $
$                            $  Advance to Corporation
$        Insurance           $
$        Company             $
$   Policy Cash Values       $
$ $ $ $ $ $ $ $ $ $ $ $ $ $ $ $- Balance of Cash Value ->$ $ $ $ $ $ $ $ $ $ $ $ $ $
                              Remains Personal       $                  $
                              Tax-Deferred Asset     $    Partner A      $
                                                     $                  $
                                              $ $ $ $ $ $ $ $ $ $ $ $ $ $
```

For example, Partner A purchases a policy on Partner B and names himself as owner and beneficiary. Partner A makes an agreement (Collateral Assignment) with Aggressive, Inc. to repay any premiums advanced by the company as premium payments at the time of the insured's death, disability, or withdrawal.

Partner A agrees to pay tax on the economic benefit he or she receives as a result of the company paying the premiums. This economic benefit is traditionally measured by the lowest applicable term insurance premium offered by the insurance company.

Imagine, for example, that Aggressive, Inc. pays a $10,000 annual premium on a $500,000 permanent policy on the life of each owner. Each partner in effect receives $10,000 annually from the company to be used to pay premiums on a policy he or she personally owns. The $10,000 "advance" is not considered income, however. The income tax liability is limited to the economic benefit which, assuming a 40-year-old partner, would be around $375. Under 1991 law, the tax cost would be no more than 31 percent of that, or $120 dollars. Income arbitrage results since the benefit generated is far greater than the required method of taxing it.

If an insured partner dies, in this case Partner B, the company would receive income tax-free proceeds equal to the premiums advanced, which would terminate the Collateral Assignment made between the surviving partner and the company. Partner A would receive the balance of the proceeds income tax-free. He or she would then be able to use the proceeds to complete the contractual responsibilities under the terms of the business continuation plan.

Split Dollar employs the use of a permanent life insurance policy. That means either Universal Life or Whole Life. Once again, a trusted advisor and a thorough examination of alternatives is the only way to ensure you are making the most efficient use of your insurance dollars.

More Split Dollar Magic

There is a corollary to our Split Dollar example. If neither partner dies prior to retirement, and if Partner A wished to buy Partner B's interest, the earnings within the permanent life insurance policy in excess of the premiums advanced are available to Partner A to use as a down payment for this purchase.

Let's assume that both Partner A and Partner B choose to retire at the same time because the next generation is stepping into the picture. Whatever the reason, it requires termination of the Split Dollar arrangement. Here lies the real magic of Split Dollar.

Partner A makes a withdrawal from his or her permanent life insurance policy equal to the premiums advanced over the previous years by the company. This withdrawal is tax-free because life insurance is the only financial tool that allows withdrawals under FIFO Accounting (First In, First Out).

Partner A uses the money to repay the company for its premium advances, thus terminating the Collateral Assignment. The balance of the money, Partner A's "split" of this permanent policy, is likely to be substantial after a number of years. This represents a personal tax-deferred cash asset that Partner A can use to supplement retirement income needs.

Salary Continuation—Frosting on the Cake

Finally, we should explore one additional concept briefly. At exactly the time Partner A was retiring from the company, as explained above, he or she wrote a check to the company in repayment of premium advances made over the years. A selective Salary Continuation (Diagram F) plan would cover that check. The intent of the Salary Continuation plan is to assure that each insured partner personally recovers money equal to the premium advances made on the Split Dollar policy he or she repaid to Aggressive, Inc.

Your advisory team should suggest drafting a Salary Continuation agreement concurrent with the Cross-Purchase and Split Dollar agreements. The basic provisions of this agreement are for Aggressive, Inc. to pay a supplemental income to Partner A at some future date, and to pay a supplemental income to Partner A's estate at some future date—in case Partner A dies before retirement. Note that no current income tax liability is created for Partner A by the promise of these future benefits.

DIAGRAM F

Executive Salary Continuation

```
$ $ $ $ $ $ $ $ $ $ $                    $ $ $ $ $ $ $ $ $ $ $
$                   $                    $                 $
$ Aggressive, Inc. $<- - - Selective - - ->$   Partner A   $
$                   $      Agreement     $                 $
$ $ $ $ $ $ $ $ $ $ $                    $ $ $ $ $ $ $ $ $ $ $
```

Basic Agreement Provisions:

1. To pay supplemental income to Partner A at some future date.
2. No current tax liability to Partner A for future benefits.
3. To pay a supplemental income to Partner A's estate at some future date in the event of his death.
4. Intent is to assure recovery of the premium portion of the life insurance policy to Partner A or his estate after split-dollar "Roll-out."

In the Event of Partner A's Death:

```
$ $ $ $ $ $ $ $ $ $ $
$                   $
$     Insurance     $
$     Company       $   Income Tax-Free
$                   $   - - - Proceeds - - ->   $ $ $ $ $ $ $ $ $ $ $
$ $ $ $ $ $ $ $ $ $ $                           $                 $
$ $ $ $ $ $ $ $ $ $ $       Tax Deductible      $ Aggressive, Inc. $
$                   $  <- - - - Dollars - - - -  $                 $
$    Partner A's    $                           $ $ $ $ $ $ $ $ $ $ $
$     Estate        $
$                   $
$ $ $ $ $ $ $ $ $ $ $
```

At Retirement of Partner A:

```
$ $ $ $ $ $ $ $ $ $ $                    $ $ $ $ $ $ $ $ $ $ $
$                   $      Pay Cash      $                 $
$ Aggressive, Inc. $- - - - Values - - - ->$    Partner A   $
$                   $     (Deductible)   $                 $
$ $ $ $ $ $ $ $ $ $ $                    $ $ $ $ $ $ $ $ $ $ $
```

Although the illustration is simplified to cover only Partner A, the same opportunity would likely be installed for all partners having significant ownership.

The funding for the plan occurs when needed—at retirement. Remember, the partners withdrew money from their permanent life insurance policies and repaid Aggressive, Inc. for the premium advances made on their behalf. Now each will begin to receive "salary continuation payments" for a time specified in the Salary Continuation plan drafted many years earlier.

Summary

Our discussion up to now has focused on concepts—specifically business continuity, split dollar, and salary continuation. These concepts, once explored and understood, can be woven together to provide the business owner a tapestry of the most efficient use of resources.

Regardless of what legal contract you use, it's absolutely necessary that business people wanting to create wealth install a Business Continuation Agreement that includes an annually updated valuation.

PLANNING HABIT 2

A Strategic Planning Short Course

"You can't hit a target you cannot see, and you cannot see a target you do not have."

— Zig Ziglar

Business planning is a term often used synonymously with strategic planning. I would like to make a distinction. Business planning is best associated with the preparation that occurs *prior to going into business*. It also occurs after the business opens, when a company is seeking extensive external financing, usually through venture capitalists.

If you are trying to raise a significant amount of capital, you will need a five-year business plan. You might want to read *Business Plans That Win Dollars* by Stanley Rich and David Gumpert. It's the best book I've found on business planning.

The emphasis of *Habits of Wealth* is to create wealth through effective entrepreneurial thinking. As a result, we deal only with Strategic Planning, typically a three-year plan with annual updates. It formalizes in writing the focus, direction, and expectations of an organization. Strategic planning, when properly executed, makes success happen.

Shortly after it became obvious our *Tri-State Neighbor* magazine would succeed, our general manager and I, with agreement of his key people, identified in our Strategic Plan when the magazine would reach one million dollars in annual revenues. We set this objective four years before the goal was achieved. We reached our million dollar objective at the planned time and immediately created a new objective for reaching the two million mark.

When a Strategic Plan is not in place, the company's direction is no clearer than an unlighted street at midnight. Vision is blurred. The company floats like a riverboat without a rudder. Without an organizational strategy, employees will design their own plan. It might be to get by with the least effort possible, participate in office politics, or give authority to an informal, self-appointed leader who lacks the information necessary to give meaningful directions. Planning is an effective antidote to these and other corporate poisons.

Strategically planned goals and objectives are the wood on the fire of success. Like wood, the plan must be occasionally replenished to keep the fire hot. Planning is a process requiring annual renewal.

Strategic planning intimidates many who attend planning seminars or read about it. It needn't be that way. The planning short course that follows is just that—a simplified, abbreviated method offering you an opportunity to get out of the starting blocks.

Many organizations prefer that an experienced facilitator walk them through their first strategic plan. That's a good idea. One thing I know for certain, having facilitated many planning sessions, is that the plan gets done that way. The initial plan has special importance, since it acts as the foundation for subsequent planning. If, after reading this Habit, you have reservations about leading an initial strategic planning session yourself, find someone qualified to help you. The return on your investment will be enormous.

Answers to Common Planning Questions

Q: How often is strategic planning done?
A: Most plans are for three years, with annual updates.

Q: When is the best time of the year to do your strategic planning?

A: You will want to have your plan completed at least one month before the beginning of the fiscal year covered by the plan.

Q: Who is involved in the planning process?

A: If your organization is small (10 or fewer employees), you might wish to include everyone. As an organization gets larger, key departmental personnel usually make up the planning team. After completion, team members familiarize other appropriate employees with the plan.

Q: How long does it take to do a Strategic Plan?

A: For companies of small to medium size the initial plan will usually take two full days to complete. Thereafter, annual updates will usually take at least one full day.

Q: How long is a completed plan?

A: For most small to medium-sized organizations the plan is between eight and 12 pages. The larger the organization, the longer the plan.

SIMPLIFIED STRATEGIC PLAN OUTLINE FOR AGGRESSIVE, INC.

I. Definition

II. Introduction

III. Develop Purpose and Mission Statements

IV. Develop Organizational Goals, Objectives, and Measurements

SAMPLE FACILITATOR'S OUTLINE FOR AGGRESSIVE, INC.

I. *Definition*: Strategic planning is the identification and creation of the most advantageous conditions possible within which to employ the art and science of goal management.

II. *Introduction*: The quality of decisions, plus their appropriateness and timing, will determine the success of your organization. An effective planning process provides the basis for better decision making. Thus, planning is an integral and vital part of any achieving organization. Strategic planning is also known as directional planning. This is appropriate since strategic planning seeks to determine the direction an organization will take.

Aggressive, Inc. is currently placing major emphasis on the development of the strategic planning process, from which will flow our yearly planning. The success of our planning is highly dependent upon the involvement of Aggressive, Inc. staff. The benefits will include:

1. *Creating* a clear, written communication which will serve as a continuous reference point for our strategic direction.

2. *Allowing* participation of several key individuals in charting the direction of our organization.

3. *Developing* anticipatory thinking, serving to help Aggressive, Inc. be more proactive.

4. *Establishing* formal, written, and consistent strategies to direct our meeting agendas, and to provide an annual mechanism for the updating of these strategies.

III. *Purpose and Mission Statements*: Part One of the strategic planning process consists of developing the Purpose and Mission Statements. The purpose statement should answer the question, "What do we want to accomplish?" We want to gain an overall perspective of Aggressive, Inc.'s direction. We want to state the scope of our involvement. This scope describes the needs of the marketplace we are serving.

Purpose Statement Overview:

—"What do we want to accomplish?"

—Might start with "To provide" or "To achieve"

—Very broad, very conceptual

—One paragraph

Sample Purpose Statement:
"To achieve market dominance and higher profitability through an aggressive, proactive, and opportunistic entrepreneurial effort by becoming leaders in the areas of customer delight, local store marketing, media planning, and employee relations."

The Mission Statement further defines our scope and provides an overview of "Why does Aggressive, Inc. exist?" It also describes long-term growth direction.

Mission Statement Overview:
—"Why does Aggressive, Inc. exist?"
—Statement might start with "To promote" or "To succeed"
—Two to four single sentence paragraphs

Sample Mission Statement:
The mission of Aggressive, Inc. is:
1. *To provide* customer delight by creating an obsession for exceeding customer expectations.
2. *To maximize* profitability by establishing and effectively implementing guidelines and follow up procedures to insure our high standards of excellence are met in all areas of operations.
3. *To increase* revenues by providing positive and efficient marketing communications that create retention and expansion of our customer base.

IV. *Organizational Goals, Objectives and Measurements*:

Goals:
This is Part Two of the planning process. Our goals, which should start with a "To be" statement, deal with developing between two and five brief conceptual statements.

Goals Overview:
Normally expressed in two to five brief conceptual sentences.

Starts with *to be*

Sample Goals:
1. *To be* the best in providing customer delight.
2. *To be* the industry leader in same-store unit sales growth.
3. *To be* viewed as the best place to work within our industry in our market area.
4. *To be* a highly entrepreneurial organization, constantly challenging ourselves to look for and be receptive to change and opportunities.
5. *To be* successful financially, achieving our stated revenue and profit margin goals.

Objectives and Measurements:
Organizational objectives should consist of six to 14 *to do* statements. These objectives relate to specific items we want to achieve as a part of our job description.

The last portion of Part Two of our planning process involves measuring our objectives. Each objective will have one, two, three, or more related measurements. These measurements, which answer the "what we will do and when" question, are a means of stating what actions will be taken to assure the objectives are met, and by what date.

Organizational Objectives:
Usually six to 14 *to do* statements.

Measurements for Objectives:
One, two, three, or more *will do's* per objective, stating who will be responsible to do them and by when.

Sample Organizational Objectives
with Accompanying Measurements

Sample Objective:
Human Resource Manager to monitor and improve employee retention.

Sample Measurements:

A. *To maintain* monthly co-worker, manager, assistant manager, and corporate turnover rates at less than 1.5 percent and to publish these figures on a monthly basis.

B. *To provide* a monthly summary measuring the percent of co-workers longevity by the following levels: Less than one year, one to two years, two to three years, and over three years.

C. *To implement*, on a semi-annual basis, a full-day, off premises operational meeting with managers. The first meeting to be held by May 31.

Sample Objective:

To effectively pursue new accounts and increase sales among current accounts.

Sample Measurements:

A. *Sales staff* to open 120 new accounts during the year.

B. *General Manager* to develop a new account letter by June 1, to be sent to all new accounts.

C. *Sales Manager* to monitor personal sales calls to assure all customers are visited in person at least three times each year.

D. *Sales Manager* to develop three new account promotions during the year, with the first in place by April 20.

E. *Sales staff* to increase our forward contracts by $100,000 during fiscal 12 months.

What to Do When the Plan Is in Place

The success of your Strategic Plan depends on the frequency and consistency of its use. It should be consulted weekly by responsible parties and quarterly by the planning group as a whole. It must become an integral part of the organization's fabric and personality.

Be sure your plan is carefully organized, neatly typed and appropriately covered or bound. It should be marked confidential and distributed to those who have a responsibility to carry it out.

Your plan isn't complete until you have determined "who and when" responsibility for each Objective Measurement. Specific agreement should be obtained to determine who will be responsible for implementing the measurement and by what date it will be accomplished. Be very specific at the measurement level. Don't let agreed on implementation dates slide. Follow up on your measurements continuously. They are the real heart of the effectiveness of your plan's implementation.

Summary

Trying to be an achieving leader without planning effectively is like driving at night with your lights off. You may eventually arrive safely, but not without significant and foolhardy risk. And even if you do reach your destination without an accident, you will always arrive later than competition who planned—and drove with their lights on.

You have heard it before—"If you are failing to plan, you're planning to fail." It really is more than a cliche. The road to success passes through planning. If you don't plan, your business life will be full of detours. Planning is success insurance.

PLANNING HABIT 3

Integrate Your Personal and Organizational Planning

The primary focus of this book is the creation of wealth through entrepreneurial behavior. Creating wealth is of minimum value, however, if it is not preserved. Therefore, the final planning consideration is an integrated review of personal and organizational planning. Start by thoroughly reviewing wills and trusts to assure that these personal documents are complementary to business documents prepared through the business continuation planning process.

Explore ways to optimize federal estate tax credits. Examine a Living Trust as a way to reduce or avoid probate expenses. Consider the use of an Irrevocable Trust to provide liquidity for the payment of federal estate taxes.

Most people create a will shortly after marriage, graduation from college, or before leaving for an extended trip. Most people also buy an automobile when they begin a career. Yet how many do you see driving the same vehicle years later when situations and success have changed their financial condition? Think about it. What model financial plan are you driving?

The planning information in this chapter is valuable. Take these Habits to a lawyer and insurance agent meeting our suggested selection criteria. Ask them to use this chapter as a basis for creating legal documents and funding suggestions appropriate to your needs.

Achievement creates wealth. Planning preserves it. I've implemented every wealth-creating and wealth-preserving concept discussed in this chapter. Planning has worked for me. It can work for you.

X

ENTREPRENEURIAL LIFE: UP CLOSE AND PERSONAL WITH LYNNE BYRNE

Being the life mate of a successful, achieving entrepreneur can be fulfilling and frustrating, exciting and exhausting, inspiring and overshadowing. Lynne Byrne has experienced all of these emotions. Our discussion with her covers every aspect of life: family, mental, financial, career, spirituality, social, and physical components. In this candid interview, conducted by a stranger, and with no input from Bill, she shares the other side of the coin: "The Wife Life."

I: Do you come from an entrepreneurial family?
L: No, not at all. The life of risk was a totally new experience.

I: And your mother was probably a homemaker?
L: Yes, Mom was a homemaker.

I: So this probably didn't prepare you that much for being the wife of a very go-go-go kind of guy.

L: No, and when I was growing up there was never any talk of business in our home at all. A very different situation from our home today. So from that aspect it's really a whole new ball game.

I: What has been the hardest thing for you to adjust to?

L: The continuous change in our lives. The first big change came when we'd been married just about a year, and Bill decided at 11 o'clock one night he was going to be a stockbroker. I was teaching art at the time.

He quit his job and we moved from Storm Lake, Iowa, into my parent's basement in Sioux Falls, South Dakota, while he went looking. I had trust in him and we had my $325 a month teaching salary to live on until the summer was over. His looking went on for about two months. He interviewed and interviewed and was turned down over and over. You see he was only 25 years old. About the seventh week one of the firms invited him to join them. He decided the next day to turn them down! He didn't feel they were right. Well that was . . . I mean I was just . . .

I: That would be traumatic for you.

L: Yes, it really was! I was 23 years old and wondering what have I gotten myself into? A few days later Dain Bosworth, the firm he really wanted to join, called and asked him to come to work. Bill was the youngest stockbroker they had ever hired. At 29 he became the youngest New York Stock Exchange branch office manager in the nation. He knew what he wanted.

I: Has the trauma level and adjustment gotten less hectic?

L: After 25 years of marriage, the adjusting gets easier and easier. Life used to be a lot more difficult. My life was kind of a mental roller coaster. It's still sort of a mental ride, but now more of a merry-go-round. Things are more level now.

I: This penchant of his to hold out for what he really wants, is that something he has demonstrated throughout your marriage and has it typically turned to his advantage or come around to sting him sometimes?

L: Time and time again he sets his goals and goes for them. He always dots all the i's and crosses all the t's. While he learns a great deal about what he's pursuing, sometimes it still stings him.

But the word failure isn't in our vocabulary. If something doesn't work out, and there has been some businesses that have not, it's just an opportunity to take what you have learned and use it as a springboard into another venture. That's how the *Tri-State Neighbor*, our farm and ranch magazine, came about.

We had a weekly newspaper called the *Sioux Falls Tribune* that won all kinds of national awards for design, editorial content, sports content, and photography. However, it didn't make any money! We were up against Gannett, and they don't much care for competition. That was tough. They had very deep pockets and we didn't. It was also at the time when interest rates jumped to 21 percent. Bill, being a farm boy, was searching for a new avenue. We had many talented people and state-of-the-art equipment, but it just wasn't going anywhere monetarily. So he looked around for a way to make the publishing business work and decided there was a need for a regional farm and ranch magazine.

My Iowa farm boy went off for a year in a little black Thunderbird selling advertising in a three-state area all by himself. The new idea, the *Tri-State Neighbor*, has been a tremendous success. A year later he purposely shut down the *Tribune*. If there has been something that didn't turn out the way he wanted, he has always used it as a springboard to success.

I: Was his drive evident to you when you first met him?

L: When I first met him what I liked about him most was that he was terribly clever and bright, but rather shy. We spent the first few dates trying to out-pun each other, trying to out-clever each other. I knew he was a strong person even back then. He says he knew long before I, that I was the woman he wanted to spend the rest of his life with.

I: What is your role in all this?

L: My background is teaching on the elementary level and also teaching art. If there is an artistic endeavor where I can contribute, I do. I enjoy immensely being involved in his business life. I've done newspaper photography and darkroom work for ten years. I was the chief photographer for six years for our *Tri-State Neighbor*.

We also have a number of Taco John's restaurants in Iowa. When the interiors need decorating, I get involved. I take any chance to be engrossed and I love it. There's a down-side to that, too. The down-side is when you sleep with the boss and work with the people, you walk a fine line. I have to use caution and balance. Sometimes it can be difficult.

I: Elaborate on that a little. Many women reading this book may find themselves in a similar situation. They are somewhat involved in the business, but basically it's their husband's thing. Are you saying you're perceived as an outsider by the employees?

L: No, not at all. I have never felt that I'm perceived as an outsider. Kind of the opposite. I'm a very social person. Sometimes they confide in me, tell me things they really shouldn't. They use me as a vehicle to get to Bill. When I was younger and less wise, I would bring up a problem at some inopportune hour like 10 P.M.! I learned very quickly not to discuss business problems after 6 P.M. What I have learned to do with employees is be a good listener, not really give them feedback. That's not my job. I tell them I really feel they should discuss it with Bill, or with their manager or department head. Whatever their needs or frustrations are I'm sure they will be taken care of if they verbalize them to the right people. Then I thank them for telling me and reinforce that I hope they will now share it with the proper people.

I: So you basically are a sounding board, but you don't take action. You encourage them to go back through the appropriate channels.

L: Yes. Once in awhile, depending on the situation, I will give them feedback. However, that doesn't work out well. Bill becomes very upset.

I: He feels a little betrayed probably?

L: Yes. Why didn't they come to him? Well, when you're sitting in a car with someone for two hours, they chit chat. I'm accessible. Through the years, I have learned to channel those discussions. The outcome is much cleaner.

I: Does the idea of competition come up in your marriage at all?

L: Bill is a very competitive person. He also loves change. He loves to have something new to learn and to try. I'm also very competitive. When you're married to a person like Bill there are two paths to take. You can sit back, stay at home, and raise the children. Be the sweet, loving wife, a tag along. That's a word I use to describe some situations, and one I despise. I think there is great danger to a relationship if the wife chooses this path. Bill is always pursuing new goals and new opportunities; he's growing and learning. If I would have stayed at home, not gotten involved in my own endeavors, not grown and learned, we would have drifted apart.

I've seen this cause a lot of problems in marriages. Of course, getting involved in your husband's business can be dangerous, too. You have to be very careful. I have the best of both worlds. He's great about letting me do what I want to do. He's also good about that with his employees, letting them grow.

The predominant way I have structured myself is being very involved in the arts and the community. Through the years I've taken part in major projects. I have also been deeply involved in the arts and drama at our children's schools; using my talents and interests to fulfill a need—my own need to grow and experience new challenging opportunities.

I: So you both have something interesting to bring to this relationship.

L: Yes. He's proud of what I do, too. Every woman needs to be told by her spouse that he notices and is proud of her accomplishments. On the other hand, I really want to know what's going on in his business world. I'm obviously curious, and I want to be able to talk intelligently to him. When I'm involved in a meeting I want to know what subject matter is discussed. I want to know what the background is so I can understand and ask intelligent questions. I think it's so important to keep moving at the same pace.

I: What makes him so different from most men? He's a successful entrepreneur in a place where you don't expect to find extraordinarily successful entrepreneurs.

L: First, let me surprise you. South Dakota is a very entrepreneurial state. Our town of Sioux Falls is one of the best places to live in the country . . . people just don't know about it. To the rest of the question, Bill's an achiever. He has been successful in creating and running small- and medium-sized businesses. He has always had great belief in himself. He has looked beyond our town of 100,000 for business opportunities. He's always had vision; I would say he was a futurist before the word became popular. I know he was born with raw intelligence and, obviously, drive. He has always had great confidence in what he could do. I haven't. That has caused friction in our marriage through the years. It's my problem—I understand that now. He has always been extraordinarily fair to people. Very fair, very ethical.

I: That's a nice thing to be able to say about your husband.

L: He really is; I think that's one of the things I love about him the most. He feels he can succeed, but he wants others to succeed with him. He wants others to grow and that's the best way to do it.

I: You bet. Then you've got really dedicated employees.

L: Yes. Bill has always made a point of trying to do special things for his staff—an unexpected paid day off, tickets to local arts and sports events. Perhaps more importantly, he believes in incentive rewards for performance and productivity.

I: Can you talk more about where his achieving instincts came from?

L: Way back when we were sophomores in college he was interested in franchising. Just fascinated with the concept. On a date, we'd go to some of those early franchise restaurants and snoop around. Since I first knew him he has been an avid reader, wanting to learn. His interest in franchising really was a seed.

During his college days he paid most of his way through college by working, sometimes full-time while going to school full-time. One of the jobs he had was with Northwestern Bell in Omaha. He quickly learned that corporate life was not for him. He didn't see achievers in the corporate structure. Everyone seemed to waste their time. He became, to use his phrase, a corporate dropout. He knew early he wanted to work for himself! When he was a stockbroker, in the world of finance, a lot of his clients were successful people. He observed and learned from them.

I: Let's talk about family life. Your daughter Jennifer just graduated from high school. Go back maybe ten years for our readers. How did you keep a balance between professional concerns and family life? And how did you serve as a catalyst to try and keep that together?

L: Both of us, and this is true of our generation—the 40- to 50-year olds—were brought up in families that found it difficult to communicate needs and feelings. It was true in my family. They loved and cared for me very much, but communication was not a two-way street a lot of the time.

That was the norm of that generation. It was also true in Bill's family to an extent. His mother was a loving and caring woman, but because of his father's problems, the family was dysfunctional. Bill, being the oldest of six, had to deal with a lot of mental trauma. He still has to deal with the ghosts of his youth. For many years I didn't understand some of his behavior. It affected our family life.

Through counseling, we have finally understood and gotten rid of some of the hurtful past. We realized from the beginning it was extremely important to have a high level of frank, two-way communication with our children. We needed to be good listeners. Bill has always been a wonderful father. There were times when he was wrapped up in business affairs, traveling and so on. But I didn't have to work an 8 to 5 job out of the home. It was a blessing I could always be there for our kids. He has been very supportive. We wanted to be the parents who enjoyed having their kids' friends around. Let them feel welcome.

If there was a crisis situation—a divorce or a teen pregnancy—we would discuss it. We would talk about the ramifications, how many people would be touched by this event. We would always talk about ways to prevent these hurtful occurrences. In so doing, we thought these discussions would help them make better choices and avoid some pitfalls as they travel through life.

I: Do you think Jason and Jennifer ever felt jealous of the business? Did they ever feel like Dad was gone too much and, yeah, you're here Mom—but I want to talk to Dad or I want to do something with Dad. Or he's not here for this or that event?

L: Yes, there was an element of that. Bill does a lot of his work at home. He might have been there physically, but he wasn't there mentally. To this day that is a problem. He isn't a workaholic, but he's a thinkaholic. We'll be eating dinner—which we have always tried to do together. The family will be having a discussion and Bill will be off on Mars someplace. We used to just get ticked off, now we tell him our needs. We tell him, "Hey, we want you here. We want you in this discussion. Listen to us." He has always tried to get to the games and the events. If he's in town he's there.

I: Have you ever really had to struggle financially? If so, what did that feel like?

L: We started a group of sandwich shops while we were also funding the *Sioux Falls Tribune*. Both businesses were started with interest rates at eight percent. Shortly after we got going interest rates went nuts—they zoomed to a sickening 21 percent! That threw us a real curve ball. It was a difficult time. We had big loans and the businesses, because of the recession, were not meeting the projections. Times were very tough. Mentally, very difficult for Bill. I remember once I couldn't find him in the middle of the night. He was walking up and down the darkened street.

I: What was your approach to being the good wife during those times?

L: I was probably more frightened than he was because I had never seen him emotionally out of control. He's such a strong person. The realization that he was really frightened scared me!

As it happened, though, Bill was one of the owners of Orange Julius International. They had bought the company many years before. Another national company came along and wanted to buy Orange Julius International for a nice profit. It couldn't have been better timing for us. We took that profit and paid off some of the debt. Somebody was watching out for us.

I: How do you view the financial independence you have today?

L: I'm very thankful for it. Some days it just doesn't seem real that we have achieved as much as we have. On the other hand, the strongest response is the good feeling that you are aware there are scores of people that have been employed, are receiving good wages and are advancing into a better financial situation because of the businesses that Bill has created.

We haven't changed that much personally. We live in the same house we've lived in for 20 years. We've put on a couple of additions, but our lifestyle hasn't changed that much. We do have a home in Colorado that we love to escape to.

I: One of the thoughts that comes to me is that it's not so much the money or the things, it's the ability to do whatever one wants to do, naturally within some parameters. The ability perhaps to help other people. Say you hear of somebody who needs $5,000 to do something, and it's a valid cause. Wouldn't it be great to be able to just hand them that $5,000!

L: Oh yes, we do that. It is a wonderful feeling. A fire that destroyed several social services that need help to recover, a young person who must have scholarship money to afford college, an elderly woman who doesn't have the funds to buy her medication or new shoes—there are so many just needs.

It's a great feeling to be able to help. We both feel very deeply that we have been blessed and the more we have the more we need to share it to help others. And we do it, as the Bible says, in a low key way. As far as being able to do anything we want to do, we can't. Bill is starting new projects and there are money needs continually.

I: And there are risk factors.

L: That's true. But the risk is much less than years ago. Bill takes very calculated risks. He would never risk all of our financial security on a new venture.

I: He doesn't flippantly just jump into something?

L: No. He would never want us to have a financial setback that would ruin us. You know some people do risk the farm every time they try a new venture.

I: That's almost like gambling. For some people, it's the risk that's the fun of it, rather than the potential.

L: He's a risk-taker, but a calculated risk-taker—which is comforting. Another aspect is the children and finances. That's a difficult one.

I: A good point. How do you let your children know they're loved, but not spoil them to the point that they're little brats nobody wants to be around. Or coddle them so much they can't function as coping adults later?

L: Bill and I both grew up in families where there was little extra money. We feel that it's just so important that our kids understand that we worked hard for 25 years to achieve what we have. And that we've done it above board, we've done it ethically. But it has taken a long time. Because we do discuss business matters at home, they have always been aware and cognizant of both successes and the times that have not been successful. They see that aspect of it and see the hard work, the emotional and mental energy, that goes into achieving. They understand when they go out into the world they're going to be on their own and they're not going to have a nest egg to start off with. We feel strongly about that. We've seen situations where too much money hurts the child long-term.

I: You don't see them being part of the work? They have no interest in that?

L: Jennifer is undecided. Jason has a great interest in working with his dad, and Bill feels very happy and proud that Jason wants to. Lots of kids don't want anything to do with their family business. Jason knows we will welcome him into the companies. First, however, he must go someplace else for two or three years after college. Do it on his own. Both kids need to be off on their own, to discover and learn in their own space.

I: That's a wise approach because then he'll come in with fresh insight, too.

L: Yes. And maybe he'll never come back to work in the family businesses. Maybe he'll discover other opportunities he wishes to pursue. If he or she come right back to the nest from college, they may never know what else was out there. That's the way we are going to handle that aspect of parenting.

Since our kids' early teens, they have had checking accounts and savings accounts. They earn money monthly. A percentage must go into their savings account. Their financial needs—school meal tickets, haircuts, clothes, etc.—they are responsible for. They learn the value of a dollar a lot quicker if they are given the task of managing their own funds. It has worked very well.

I: Do you ever feel jealous of the business?
L: Yes, when a new project is being put together I would like to be more involved. The most jealous I have ever been was during the writing of this book. It was his mistress. We've only had two mistresses in our marriage—golf and this book. It consumed him. He used to have a five handicap in golf. When he decided to write the book, he knew he would plunge into it totally, so he stopped golfing completely!

He knew he had to go off, shut the door and just do it. The first couple of weeks I hated it. He had his nose in that damned word processor all day long, every day, every night, every weekend. After a couple of weeks I thought to myself, "Come on, snap out of this and busy yourself with something you can be consumed in, too." I just needed to focus on my own interests. Then I was okay.

I: You realized it was not a forever thing?
L: Yes. I handled it. I wanted him to do it and I was proud of him for attempting it, but I didn't like the fact I wasn't getting any attention. Whenever he starts a new project, all his energy is focused. If he keeps me informed then I'm fine.

I: You sound like a pretty reasonable person. If you know what his goals are and what his methodology is to reach them, then you can assess that and work around it.
L: I have many interests of my own I can pursue.

I: Which, with this kind of man, would almost be a necessity. Otherwise you would become a Dolly Domestic who's of no interest to him at all.

L: You wouldn't be around long. I mean, you would hate him and he would hate you.

I: How do you and Bill find time for social life?

L: Our social life has evolved around sports and our children. Bill travels a great deal so many times he can't attend functions we are invited to. I go by myself usually. It used to bother me to even go to a show by myself. It doesn't anymore.

I: Do you take family vacations? Do they work?

L: Before and after a trip is a very stressful time for Bill. One has to tread lightly, kind of like avoiding the "occasion for confrontation." Remind the kids several times, don't put any extra added stress on dad's shoulders.

We have taken many family vacations. We all have fond memories of the great places we've experienced together. Bill is able to leave the office because he has always empowered his people. They can get along and go about their business without his presence.

In the last five years he has gotten into the habit of taking his fax along and working half days on some trips. This can be disruptive for everyone. He wants the kids quiet. The kids want dad to relax and enjoy. We started to discuss, before leaving for a vacation, what the situation was going to be. If the ground rules are set and understood by all before the trip begins, all will have a better time. If Dad wants to work from six to 10 every morning, then the rest of the family will not bug him. But Dad must abide by the schedule too. At 10 A.M. the fax and phones are put away for the rest of the day and he enters the vacation "mindset."

I: Do you go with him very often when he travels?

L: I will in the future. I really did not want to leave the kids much. I didn't feel it was fair to them. When they were in their teens I would have someone they could relate to stay with them, a college friend or a young professional person who was a family friend. They were much happier with someone like that than with a 70-year-old lady! Now that we are empty nesters, I'll travel with him a lot more.

I: How does success change your social lives?

L: Because Bill is a high achiever and has had many successes, there are certain things that happen socially which hurt. You become separated from some of your old friends. They remain at the same level they were 10 years ago in their business or financially. Some simply don't feel comfortable with us now. In a few cases, others are jealous of Bill's achievements and that creates a barrier.

I: Do you have some dear friends who you can discuss it with?

L: Yes, and that helps.

I: Your observation says a lot about our society: that we're preoccupied with social climbing or monetary acquisition, as opposed to the humanness in people.

L: It's really too bad but that's just the way it is. When financial status changes, relationships change. There is a perception that people who have money have lots of friends. However, the truth is many times it causes the *loss* of dear old friends. Some people are uncomfortable. Others resent success. Bill is a different animal in a business sense, too. He's always doing something new and exciting—most people aren't. They are just maintaining. He's very creative and intense. That's tough for people to handle. However, we do keep meeting interesting new people around the country with whom we have many things in common.

I: So the social life is more of an evolving thing.

L: It really does evolve, yes.

I: Do you try to mix business and pleasure or purposely keep them apart?

L: We don't mix the two. Until recently our business customers were outside the town where we live. The restaurants are in Iowa, and the magazine does business in a seven or eight state area. Now we have a new division of The Byrne Companies—a human resources development division—so we have entered a new era as far as doing business in our community. I'm sure some of our friends will use our services to better their companies and the growth of their people. It is a new door opening. I really don't think that we will ever mix the two. If I'm having a dinner party or a barbecue, I don't sit down and make calculating lists of who should be invited. I've never thought that way, and Bill sure doesn't.

I: I know you've shared a lot about using your artistic talents. Are there other things that you do to stay mentally stimulated? Any courses you take?

L: Yes, I have taken many courses. I am a right-brained person—emotional, sensitive and spontaneous. Bill is a left-brained person—logical, mathematical, analytical. Opposites attract. It can, however, cause big problems if you are not on the same track when you are trying to communicate. If I am looking at a problem emotionally and Bill is looking at the same problem logically we will never get anywhere. I have to jump into his logical mode or he has to jump into my emotional mode. That way we can talk the same language.

There are areas of his life that are Greek to me. Take accounting. He created an accounting system 15 years ago for our restaurants that a CPA told him was ingenious. That kind of stuff is second nature to him. It doesn't come naturally to me at all. For years it bothered me that I didn't understand the terms, the how-to, of accounting. Recently I took an accounting course at a local college. I feel so much better knowing the terminology. Now I understand it when I hear it or see it. I should have done that years ago!

If there is an area of knowledge that a husband uses in his business life and the wife doesn't understand it, she should find a way to learn about it. I don't think the husband's the one to teach her. Go out and take some courses. So many of the people in adult education these days are non-traditional students; you don't feel like everyone's mom. There will likely be several people in the class your age.

I: You have a whole new competence level that you've never had before.

L: Yes. I wish I would have taken that course 15 years ago instead of feeling inadequate about it all these years. I recently took a personality profile that The Byrne Companies markets. I got an excellent on my business terminology. Bill just about did a flip. I told him before the accounting class, I wouldn't have known one of the terms.

I: You sound like you have just as much determination as he does.

L: You have to, to coexist with somebody like that.

I: Do you think he's pretty realistic in giving you and the kids the time you've needed? How does a wife help a husband do this if he's a very busy achiever?

L: Bill is a perfectionist. He expects everyone to do their best. Sometimes that can cause problems in the family. There is a term paper that one of the kids showed Dad. It's a 96 percent—a darned good effort. He'll tell them it's a good job, but then he'll start correcting it . . . "If you did this, or if you did that." He is trying to be helpful, but it can rub the wrong way. There has to be a balance. A wife or child can feel inadequate pretty fast if positive vibes always end with a suggestion of how something could have been done better.

Sometimes he would treat us like his staff. He's got a wonderful staff. These people are at his beck and call at the office. He used to come home sometimes and treat his wife and family like staff. That didn't go over very well. In the last few years it has changed because, as a family, we've addressed the problem and communicated our feelings and needs to him. He is now conscious of the fact family and staff are treated differently.

I: How do you handle it when Bill works at home?
L: If I have something I need to discuss with him and I can see he is mentally preoccupied, I tell him I need to talk to him. In essence I make a date to talk to him. It might be in five minutes or an hour. At the appointed time both of us are ready to give each other their undivided attention.

I: How important is the spiritual connection in your life?
L: Both of us were raised Roman Catholics. Our faith has always been very important to us. We've always prayed together and gone to church together as a family. We feel very deeply about our faith, and we know if we ask— strength, wisdom, or whatever will be provided.

I: On a scale of one to 10, 10 being the highest, where do you feel that comes in?
L: A nine.

I: How much do you think where you are now is reflective of that?
L: The way we have raised our family is greatly reflected. In the business world, Bill's deep sense of right and wrong has made a great difference. Neither of us is afraid to speak up and share our views on the importance of our spiritual life.

I: Does it feel good to have the wisdom and the courage to reach out and sort of minister to others?
L: Several times when I have seen friends having difficulty I will suggest they pray about it or go to church together. Five years ago I couldn't have said that to friends. It's hard to say. I truly believe it, however. I feel our spiritual life has a great deal to do with our professional and family success.

I have a good friend, Sandy Jerstad, who has always had the gift of talking about her spirituality in a lovely, natural fashion. Listening to her and observing her has made it much easier for me to verbalize how I feel about my faith. Don't thump the Bible. Drop a gentle hint.

I: What is the greatest advantage of being the wife of a successful entrepreneur?

L: I guess I've never really looked at it in that light. I look at it in the light that I'm very happy to be married to the man I'm married to. The fact that he is successful is a bonus. Harmony is the most important word in the English language to me. I'm happy for the harmony in our lives.

Bill's achievement is advantageous. I've seen lots of interesting places, met many fascinating people—my world has mushroomed with experiences. Friends will say, "Well, what are you guys up to now? You lead the most interesting, exciting lives." We truly do!

I: The life of a busy entrepreneur could be a real detriment. It could turn harmony upside down.

L: All of us need to work at keeping our marriages in harmony. We both make a great effort to keep things smooth. At times it is difficult. He can be very intense. I tell him to go take a walk or a bike ride and calm down.

I: Let's talk about stress. People in business for themselves tend to have a high stress factor. What do you folks do to keep that under control? Does it seem to be a problem? Perhaps the other things you have in your life—such as your spiritual connections and your very "together" marriage—maybe that helps to negate a lot of the stress.

L: Those factors help; but it certainly doesn't negate all of it. Bill's mom died of malignant hypertension, which is blood pressure out of control, when she was 45 years old. It was three months before our wedding. Her mother-of-the-groom dress was delivered to their farm the day of her funeral. Eleven years ago Bill drove himself to the hospital, thinking he was having a heart attack. By the end of that scary week we knew he had not had a heart attack. The culprit was hypertension. We knew if he wanted to live a long, healthy life he had to change his lifestyle.

Emphasis was placed on eating correctly, cardiovascular exercise and stress management. We've been on a regimented exercise program since 1980. We exercise every other day, five miles on our Schwinn Airdyne stationery bike, jogging, walking or hiking. Bill encourages his staff to exercise by offering a health club membership to them.

I: What a wonderful stress reducer.

L: It's great! He'll come home after a wild day, get on his Airdyne and the stress just comes rolling off.

I: Although you're obviously very competent and seem a complete person, I'm sure at times you must feel overshadowed.

L: Oh, yes. Change is second nature to Bill, I relate to change differently, as many people do. It is difficult for me. I have learned not to be afraid of it. I still am not as comfortable with it as he is . . . never will be.

Several years ago I felt terribly overshadowed and unable to cope with his intensity and other aspects of his personality. I simply couldn't tolerate it anymore. Of course, at that time I thought it was all his fault. I told him we had to seek professional help.

Friends had mentioned a specific counselor who had helped them. I had kept his name, sensing that eventually we were going to need a good counselor. We were very fortunate to have a gifted, caring man who helped us learn about ourselves. The problems were half mine and half Bill's. I remember the counselor saying, "Well, now what if he doesn't change? Are you going to divorce him?" I said, "No, I love him." "What are you going to do?" he said. I didn't know what I was going to do!

Bill reacted to my request for counseling in a manner similar to how he reacts to other opportunities for change or improvement—very positively. His attitude towards change keeps him looking forward, towards learning, towards bettering our lives. That's one of the benefits of living with an achieving-type person. There are often problems, but they're not as set in their ways, and in this situation that was a real asset.

During our counseling, and after spending two or three hours alone with Bill and learning about his philosophies and ideas, our counselor asked Bill if he had ever thought about writing a book. Over the years several others had mentioned that too. Anyway, our counselor's suggestion was quite instrumental in convincing Bill he really did have a book in him. Funny how what we see as problems are often really opportunities—chances to learn and grow. It was another one of the springboards I mentioned earlier.

I worked on the roots of my feelings of inadequacy and Bill worked on his problems. It was exhausting for both of us. We were both very determined to make our lives more copacetic. We were successful in working through the problems and our relationship is more understanding and loving now than it ever was. It was tough to admit the problems and hard to seek help. But we did and we have overcome.

I: What is the most exciting future plan you have?

L: The human resource division that is now a part of The Byrne Companies. Bill is at the point in his life where he has learned a great deal, and he wants to give back. That's why he is getting into human resource work. That's why he wrote the book. That's why he has been speaking on college campuses. That's why he wants to speak to major conventions. He really wants to give something back. So many speakers have never experienced what they talk about.

We're very excited about this new company. Bill thinks it will be a huge area of need this decade, although most people don't realize it yet. It's futuristic! I'm hoping to become more involved in this new endeavor; it's very exciting.

I: If you could go back in time what would you do differently?

L: I would deal with all those frustrations I've lived with regarding my relationship with Bill and our family. I would have had less pride and less arrogance to think that I could handle some of these problems by myself. I would've sought professional help earlier to avoid all those painful times.

I: Do you have more advice for entrepreneurial wives?

L: If you want to maintain a close relationship with your mate and expect him to confide in you concerning business matters, some being very private matters, keep his trust. He may have told you something you perceive as not really too important. This happened to me.

I went to lunch with the girls and said something about a bit of information. By the next week, it came back to haunt me. Two negative things happened. His confidence level in me took a nose dive. Part of our relationship was shut off for awhile. I was guilty of this sin, and I wish I hadn't been.

Another idea is to maintain your own support group. Achievers, because of their nature, are often loners. I need people. I am blessed with a group of women friends who are the core of a defunct bridge club. We have a network of "mental knitting" that has gone on for 20 years. They are my sounding board, my idea people, my safety net, and my great friends. Form a luncheon club or a birthday club. Find the right mix of women where you can feel safe and talk on any subject. Nurture your friendships; they become more precious as the years go by.

AFTERWORD

You made it! Congratulations and thanks for taking time to read *Habits of Wealth.*

Now I'd like to turn the tables. It's your turn to write. What habits were the most relevant to you? The least relevant? What would you like to learn more about? What ideas do you have that could be included in future writings or training sessions?

Hope to see you as I speak around the country. If we can help, let us know. And remember, it's your turn to write.

Bill Byrne
The Byrne Companies
PO Box 90225
Sioux Falls, SD 57105-0225

INDEX

goals 166-67
service effectiveness
157-67
telephone 155-56

D

Dain Bosworth 280
Debt 235 (*See also* Risk)
Decentralization 112-13, 173
Deferred compensation plan
diagram 123
non-qualified 121-23
Delegation 110-11, 134-39
levels of 137-38
MBA (Managing by
Being Away) 135
transitional 135-36
Dolly Madison handshake
146
Downey, Helen 220
Downsizing 114, 182
Dreams 7, 231-33
Drucker, Peter 169

E

Education 240-44
Effectiveness 32, 74, 157,
276
Efficiency 62, 72-74
Emerson, Ralph Waldo 197,
247
Employee Profit Ownership
Plan (EPOP) 126-27
(*See also* Sales Support
Incentive)
Empowerment 110-13, 125,
135, 161, 174
Entrepreneur's Credo, The
252
Entrepreneurial achiever

(*See also*
Achievement) 2-
10, 34, 51-52, 110
132-38, 169-70,
174, 224-26, 234,
252, 254
Environmentalist, Working
189
Equity
employee perspective
115-17
employer perspective
118-20
inequity of 115-22
tax deferred perspective
121-22
Essential self 218-19
Ethics 8, 56, 79, 105, 186,
243, 250 (*See also*
Fairness)
Evaluation 81-82, 95
Executive Bonus 263
(*See also* Split Dollar
Concept)
Exercise 230
Expectations 52, 95-98, 147,
151-52, 158-60, 172,
209, 212, 226

F

Failure 10, 52, 69, 243, 281
Fairness 7, 40, 52, 120, 132,
212, 284
Feeling/Thinking 210-11
Financial quicksand 15-16
Financial statements 18, 24,
46, 71
Financing 269
Focus 36, 239
Following/Leading 222-23